CONTE

MASTERING CHATGPT FOR BEGINNERS

HOW TO HARNESS THE POWER OF AI
LANGUAGE MODELS FOR YOUR PERSONAL
AND PROFESSIONAL GROWTH

SHANE CORBITT

FREE BONUS

Thank you for reading this book. I hope you find it insightful and helpful.

To help my readers, I've put together this FREE ChatGPT Prompt Guide.

>> Click here to get your bonuses <<

INTRODUCTION

On a fine Sunday morning, Clark logged into his computer. He was browsing the internet, desperately searching for an idea that he could use for his next big YouTube video when suddenly an email notification popped up. It read:

"Class Assignment Due Tonight: Must Submit By 11:59 PM"

It was 2 PM already, and Clark hadn't even started. He had no idea what he'd write about, nor did he prepare anything for the all-important assignment beforehand. To make matters worse, this assignment would contribute directly to his overall grades by the end of the semester.

"I need to get this done, but how?"

Clark started asking his friends to see if someone could help him write a 2,000-word assignment on some kind of a topic. While most excused themselves, one of them suggested, "Why not hire someone to do it for you?" After a quick dash through Fiverr and other freelancing platforms, Clark realized he couldn't afford to pay someone that much. If only there were a way to find assistance without paying anything in return... Well, Clark's luck was about to change.

As he searched for "how to write a 2,000-word assignment on a topic for free" on Google, something called ChatGPT popped up. It said, "Harness the power of AI and bring your ideas to life."

"Sounds interesting. I'll give that a go."

After a quick sign-up, he typed in the same search query as before. The cursor blinked before it started typing out a response faster than he could read. Before he knew it, it laid out the steps he would need to take before he was able to write anything.

"That's a lot of work. I don't have that much time."

With that, he decided to type, "Can you help me write this assignment?" Artificial Intelligence (AI) suddenly responded positively.

"Sure, I can help you with a 2,000-word assignment on artificial intelligence. However, I'll need some specific details about the assignment. What is the topic of the assignment, and what are the instructions or guidelines given by your instructor? Please provide me with these details, and I'll be happy to assist you further."

He provided the details, and his entire project was laid out in less than 2 minutes. All he did was rephrase the ideas, and he was good to go. That semester, he ended up scoring an A.

Clark's story is one of millions. Every day, ChatGPT caters to over 10 million queries, and this number is rapidly increasing (Ruby, 2023). If that isn't proof of just how powerful ChatGPT is, let me give you some more numbers:

- As of March 2023, ChatGPT has over one billion users.
- It is expected to fetch a revenue of over $200 billion by the end of 2023.
- Around 88% of the traffic that visits ChatGPT is direct.

Needless to say, AI is here to stay. More specifically, ChatGPT is just getting started. It is at the forefront, the torch-bearer of just how powerful AI can be. What you are looking at here, ladies and gentlemen, is the future, quite literally. This, then, brings us to a very important question:

"Should we be afraid of it?"

Not at all. Of course, there is the entire talk about how AI is replacing humans and how talent is now being sidelined in favor of AI, but let's not jump to conclusions right away. ChatGPT is, after all, created by human beings for fellow human beings. It is meant to assist people in finding more efficient ways to boost productivity and explore new possibilities and avenues that were not possible before.

There have been many success stories posted all over social media. ChatGPT played a vital role in all of them. It helped people explore new ideas, assisted them with the legwork, and allowed many entrepreneurs, business owners, and other professionals to do so much more without the additional cost it would incur otherwise.

As long as you are able to understand how to harness the power of AI, there is nothing to worry about. Change is good, but with every change, there are those who resist it. Back in the days when emails came in, people laughed at the idea and claimed no one would use such a thing. Today, just a few decades in, everyone uses emails and social media.

What Will You Get From Reading This Book?

Glad you asked that question. I have seen many other books and realized just how hard they can be to read, digest, and understand. Many professionals may not have the technical knowledge and may be unfamiliar with basic terms like cognitive computing, clustering, and logistic regression. Books that are not reader-friendly leave their readers confused and baffled. If a book cannot explain things easily to everyone, it fails to be a book, period.

My objective, however, is different. I wanted to write this book to help everyone understand what ChatGPT is and how they can master it to be ahead of the curve. In today's fast-paced world, you either stay ahead of the curve and be an early adopter or lag behind for the rest of your life. My goal is to ensure that the latter doesn't happen for you. Therefore, by reading this book, you'll be in a comfortable position to use ChatGPT for your professional and personal needs.

Throughout the book, I will aim to steer clear of complicated words so that everyone has an equal opportunity to learn. There will be examples, stories, facts, and much more to show how ChatGPT can be used. Furthermore, where necessary, any technical term used will be thoroughly explained so that you don't have to leave this book, log on to Google and go through an hour-long YouTube video to understand what I'm talking about. I assure you, this is going to be very easy.

Through this book, you will gain access to:

- Step-by-step guidance on crafting effective prompts that yield optimal results.
- Insider tips on controlling output length and quality for more precise and focused responses.

- Techniques for managing ChatGPT's behavior, enabling you to align the generated content with your goals and needs.
- Best practices for ensuring content safety and ethical considerations while using ChatGPT.
- Practical examples demonstrating various personal and professional applications of ChatGPT.
- Time-saving strategies for using ChatGPT to streamline content creation, research, and communication tasks.
- Insights into advanced techniques like fine-tuning ChatGPT for specific use cases, which will help you further optimize the AI's performance.
- Expert advice on integrating ChatGPT with other tools and platforms to enhance your overall productivity.
- A curated list of resources and support materials that will empower you to quickly and effectively implement the skills and techniques acquired through this book.

What Makes Me the Authority?

For quite some time, I've been using ChatGPT and understanding how things work. I, too, was once plagued by the fear that AI would ultimately replace me. However, over the years that I invested in researching and understanding AI, I realized it wasn't the case. My fears were baseless. Human beings are always going to be better than AI or ChatGPT. With that said, there are areas where people tend to grow complacent. That is human nature. In such cases, AI can come in to strengthen the team and help the business overcome such issues.

You may have explored websites where you were greeted by a chatbot. Even though you know it is just a programmed robot speaking, the fact is that it is often time-saving. When people aren't working, websites and businesses leave AI to handle chat queries and dial in answers that it can then provide to the customers so that they have some answers with them. It is just a good way of ensuring the business continues to serve around the clock.

I've seen people talk about AI while working in Sales. They were petrified by the idea of AI rendering them obsolete. The fact is that most of the job positions, if not all, require decision-making that no AI can replicate. What it can do, however, is use the data provided to it to work out the best-case scenarios and compelling pitches, and that's it. It cannot interact with another human being the way we do because no such technology can do that. Therefore, the real fear is nothing more than hatred and resistance to accept change.

After using ChatGPT and seeing firsthand the power of AI for a long time, I have found myself to be in a position where I can help fellow readers and professionals understand how to use AI to their advantage. I've been doing that for quite some time now, but my approach was limited as I was only able to help a particular number of people at once. Through this book, however, I intend to overcome that limitation and help the masses harness the power of AI and ChatGPT. By the end of this book, my goal is to ensure that readers know:

1. What ChatGPT is?
2. How to use the power of AI.
3. How to overcome and manage problems.
4. How to explore new possibilities.

To do that, we will not only learn more about ChatGPT, but I will also be taking you through some practical examples so that you get a firsthand experience of how to use it for different situations. The more you practice, the better you become at it. With that said, let's dive right into the world of ChatGPT and learn how to master it, and we do that by first understanding ChatGPT.

1

CHATGPT 101—THE ULTIMATE BEGINNER'S GUIDE

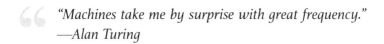 *"Machines take me by surprise with great frequency."*
—*Alan Turing*

Have you ever wondered where this popular ChatGPT came from? Who invented it, and why? And what on earth is GPT? Well, to understand all of that, we must first dive deep into the world of ChatGPT and explore its origin. This chapter is recommended for every beginner that intends to understand ChatGPT better. If you're an advanced user, you may want to skip this.

The Origin of ChatGPT

To many, it is an artificial intelligence project developed by OpenAI, the team that gave the world this powerful tool. However, that alone isn't a proper introduction.

Chat GPT was created for one sole purpose. As per the definitions on Google, it is nothing more than a chatbot powered by artificial intelligence. It was developed by OpenAI to offer human-like responses to online customers by using something called Natural Language Processing (NLP). The chatbot was designed to use these technologies and learn through websites, articles, blogs, and other textbooks so that it was in a better position to answer queries.

Before chatGPT, chatbots were odd, to say the least. You could tell from a mile away that you were interacting with essentially a robot. The flat tone and the inability to understand questions properly often frustrated customers. Think about it this way. You visit a website where you are trying to buy a product. The card was charged, but the checkout screen says, "Card declined."

Naturally, you'd want to contact the customer representative and explain that your card was charged. You see a little icon, usually on the bottom right side of the screen, that says "Chat Now." Once you click on it, a window opens up, and you see someone typing, "Hi there. My name is Sarah. How can I help you today?"

You mentioned, "Hey, Sarah. I was buying a product and I went through your checkout process. The card was charged successfully but your checkout screen says it was declined. Can you help me?"

After a few seconds of radio silence, you get the following response.

"Sure. You can use MasterCard, Visa, American Express, or Discover cards for your payments. Alternatively, you can use PayPal or G-Pay to make your payments."

That clearly shows that this so-called chat representative didn't understand your problem at all. Instead, it just picked up on the keywords "buying," "product," and "card," and assumed you were trying to buy something but weren't too sure if your card would be accepted.

This is where ChatGPT came in. The GPT stands for Generative Pre-Trained Transformer. It is a model that OpenAi developed to help consumers gain access to more human-like responses generated by the program. Now, if someone were to put in the same query, it would sound quite literally like a human being is talking.

To give you an idea, around 53% of online users failed to recognize ChatGPT's response as an AI-generated reply (Ruby, 2023). That is a massive improvement and goes to show that this technology is more reliable.

OpenAI has been working actively on ChatGPT and improving it as much as possible. At the time of writing this book, the latest version of ChatGPT is ChatGPT-4. A major update was released just a few months ago, and the world shifted from ChatGPT-3 to the one we use today. It is overwhelming to imagine the rate at which ChatGPT is spreading because it was initially released in 2018. ChatGPT-4 was released in March 2023, and there are already over a billion users registered on it.

ChatGPT is free to use, although there is a paid version that you can use too. In most cases, the free version alone should suffice. However, there are instances where you may come across a prompt saying "ChatGPT is at capacity" when trying to log in. That generally means that it is currently handling the maximum number of users and queries that it can. Since the release of ChatGPT-4, that problem has rarely occurred.

This problem, if it were to repeat, happens only to people who are using ChatGPT for free. For larger organizations that deal with big data and have excessive data queries to work with, they can opt for the paid subscription. In such a case, ChatGPT will still function for them even when it is operating at maximum capacity.

Considering the vast number of queries taking place, it does beg the question, is this another search engine? Technically, no. ChatGPT is a chat-based model that helps users share their ideas, and, in return, it is able to maintain a conversation with them. It is able to explain things, shed light on ideas, describe art, and so much more. That is something a search engine, such as Google, cannot do.

A search engine is designed to index websites and web pages. It is used to filter through keywords and then find results that match the keywords. This is something the ChatGPT cannot do. You cannot ask ChatGPT to go and search for something online as it is a language-based model. The only source of information it has is the data that was fed to it in training. It can only provide information based on what it has learned, and that leaves room for error. There are cases where the information may already be outdated or invalidated. In such cases, it will fail to identify the change as it is yet to be trained.

At the time of writing this book, I ran a simple query to find out how latest is ChatGPT's data.

"Who won the FIFA World Cup 2022 in Qatar?"

The response I received was:

"As an AI language model, I do not have the ability to predict the future or access information beyond my knowledge cutoff date, which is September 2021. As of my knowledge cutoff date, the FIFA World Cup in 2022 had not yet taken place. The tournament was scheduled to take place in Qatar from November 21 to December 18, 2022, and the winner of the tournament is yet to be determined."

This may change later on, but the fact is that ChatGPT has limited data that it is trained on. If you were to run the same search on Google, it would easily answer "Argentina" because it is a search engine. The keywords would have already been used, indexed, and optimized, meaning that as soon as you run the query, it will match the keywords and bring up the results.

The Technology Behind ChatGPT

The entire GPT model that OpenAI worked on relies on data. Think of it as a human mind. The more information you provide, the more it learns. The entire ChatGPT revolves around AI and NLP, two key concepts worth understanding. Let's take a closer look.

Artificial Intelligence

Artificial Intelligence isn't something new. It has existed since the early days of computer programming. To give you an idea, Alan Turing, famously known for providing the world with computers, created what he called the Universal Turing Machine. He is credited for being the one to crack open the Enigma Code, a method used during the wars to send coded messages and instructions to the troops on the battlefield.

Artificial Intelligence is a way through which a computer thinks and learns like a human being. While it cannot match the capabilities of a human brain, it is still a very effective way of teaching machines how to operate and make decisions based on scenarios.

A computer cannot make a decision on its own. It is either programmed explicitly to take certain courses of action, or it is powered by AI so that it can learn from its past experience and use a new approach. The latter generally involves a lot of test runs that are termed as simulations. After thousands and thousands of test runs, it can then learn what it needs to do in a given situation.

A machine cannot adapt to new situations right away. Through AI, it can try multiple scenarios at a reasonably fast pace to determine the outcome. With each try, it will do what went right, make modifications on steps that didn't work, and it does so over and over until it achieves the result. This is done through something called Machine Learning.

Machine Learning (ML)

Machine Learning is a sub-field of AI. It is what allows the machine to learn something in the first place. Without machine learning, the only other way to teach machines something would be through hundreds of thousands of lines of code.

You may be thinking all of this is too complicated, right? Let me give you an example. I am sure you've used Netflix or Social Media. Both of them use Machine Learning Algorithms, which are essentially lines of codes programmed to take into account your browsing history, your interest, what you focus on, and the kind of content you interact with the most, and then use that data to learn. This is why whenever you open Facebook, TikTok, or Netflix, you end up finding something that is tailored to your interest. This is how the "Recommended" section works on Netflix. This is how Netflix and other platforms ensure you stick around as much as possible.

Natural Language Processing (NLP)

Did you know that computers simply cannot understand English?

"What?"

Surprised? To be honest, computers cannot understand any language on earth, whether that be Arabic, Russian, Urdu,

Spanish, or even German. The only language a computer understands is that of ones and zeros. That language is called a Binary Language, where everything is written in a series of zeros and ones. Therefore, if I were to put my age as 35 in a computer prompt, typing 35 simply wouldn't make any sense to the computer. Instead, I'd have to type the following:

100011

If I were to type "My name is Shane" in binary language, it would be something like this:

01001101 01111001 00100000 01101110 01100001 01101101 01100101 00100000 01101001 01110011 00100000 01010011 01101000 01100001 01101110 01100101

That literally says, "My name is Shane," and if I were to write in such a way, it would make no sense to anyone. This then poses a problem for us. If this is how a computer understands a command or an input, how are we supposed to ask it to do things easily? That is where NLP comes in.

The NLP technology is a way through which our words are translated into a language the computer understands, recognizes, and is then able to process, all without us having to learn the binary language. Using this technology, a program, such as ChatGPT, can easily understand what we are talking about and respond accordingly in English.

By adding all of this up, OpenAI was able to put together a program that they've come to call ChatGPT.

The GPT-4 Architecture

Every program has an architecture that it is built upon. ChatGPT is no exception to that rule.

Now, you might imagine that someone who came up with this revolutionary AI chatbot was a genius, and you'd be right. OpenAI was founded by Sam Altman and Elon Musk. Those two names alone show just how advanced ChatGPT is eventually going to be.

The first version of the ChatGPT was introduced to the public in 2018. The newly dubbed "ChatGPT" had 117 million parameters that were used to train the model. This version was able to impress the audience as it was able to go through language recognition. It was also able to carry out tasks like text completion and language modeling. No other chatbot at the time was able to do so.

With these results pouring in, it quickly became popular with the masses—that and the fact that Mr. Musk tweeted about it, which further fueled the fire. Despite being state-of-the-art, it had many limitations, chief among which were the responses it generated. They weren't that convincing, even though it was miles ahead of its competitors.

In 2019, a refined version of the same was introduced and called ChatGPT-2. This time, it had 1.5 billion parameters as compared to the minuscule 117 million of its predecessor. Naturally, this was able to impress more people than ever before. It had a far more polished output and a more realistic text response, and it was able to understand human language better. This meant that your queries had effectively more chances of being understood correctly and answered accordingly.

With its increasing popularity, ChatGPT-2 continued to set new benchmarks until, in November 2022, the game-changing Chat-GPT-3 was unveiled. This is where the world came to know about ChatGPT. This is where everything changed. If the previous version had 1.5 billion parameters, this now boasted

175 billion parameters. Safe to say, it was an unprecedented improvement. Now, people could quite literally chat with it as if they were chatting to a friend. Not just that, it was now able to handle a larger number of queries, meaning that more people were able to access it concurrently. There was also ChatGPT-3.5 which had over 175 billion parameters, although no official number was released.

In March 2023, ChatGPT-4 was released. Just like its predecessor, it, too, took a massive leap. Now, it has over 1 trillion parameters. It is hard to imagine just how much data went into training the current version of ChatGPT. However, the fact remains that it is extremely fast, quite reliable, and almost 100% human-like when it comes to generating responses.

The ChatGPT-4's architecture is based on the ChatGPT-3.5 but has been fine-tuned with massive data. This is why it is able to cater to pretty much all queries through its prompt and is able to generate a human-like response.

Now, thanks to the way ChatGPT is set up, it is able not just to take in text but also images as queries. Based on what it receives, it can deliver a human-like output. I wouldn't be wrong to say that it is capable of clearing many tests that many people cannot, just to show how intellectual and intelligent it is.

This is all because of its architecture. It is what we call a large multimodal model, which is a fancier way of saying it can learn from various modes. The current version of ChatGPT uses a transformer-style architecture for its neural network. Because of this wizardry, it is better able to understand the relationship between words in a given text. Furthermore, it also employs an attention mechanism, allowing it to know what part of the text to focus on and what to rule out as irrelevant.

How Is ChatGPT Trained Through Data?

To most of us, data is just a pile of papers or numerous spreadsheets that contain numbers and some words. We don't pay attention to it as much. However, to some, it is the new-age gold. It is what allows people to develop apps that are extremely hard to ignore, create social media platforms that keep people hooked, or come up with things like ChatGPT that are able to leave us speechless.

ChatGPT uses tons and tons of text data. It uses textbooks, articles, blogs, journals, press releases, and even Wikipedia. If I was to pile all that data in printed form, I'd need the largest building in the world to accommodate the number of papers needed, maybe more.

For humans, it will be nearly impossible to take in even half of that data, but for ChatGPT, a model based on NLP, AI, ML, and all the other things I mentioned in the previous section, it is relatively easier.

Through this vigorous training, ChatGPT learns how to use a string of text to predict what comes next. For example, if I were to type Elon, it would assume I am about to type Musk because most of the data points that way.

To give you an idea, here are some words that I typed. See if you can spot a pattern here.

Words I wrote	Following word by ChatGPT
Elon	Musk
Ice	Cream
Chill	Out
Red	Color
Black	White
United	States
Orange	Fruit
Book	Page
Jesus	Christ

In the above, it is evident that ChatGPT is using data to figure out which word is more popular as a follow-up word and then presenting it to me as an answer. This is why when I wrote Ice, I hoped it would write "Land" instead of "cream."

As I said earlier, ChatGPT uses the words you put in and then predicts the best answer based on the data it was trained with. To put it in simpler terms, it isn't actually answering you; it's just recalling the popular follow-up word selection.

ChatGPT works this way because it is trained with a few ground rules. With those in mind, it is put through different situations or given a lot of data to learn from and then develop its own algorithm. Either way, it learns the patterns, assigns meaning, and then successfully predicts the plausible follow-up text. It does so through a process called "tokenization."

Tokenization

Do not confuse this for some kind of an NFT or cryptocur-rency-related thing. Tokenization, as far as ChatGPT goes, is a process through which the program breaks the text down into smaller bits. By doing so, it ends up creating tokens.

Many words often lead to a single token, but they can have multiple tokens if the sentences are complex or longer. If we were to take an average, most tokens are just four characters long (characters include whitespace).

Since we humans write all the text, ChatGPT's AI breaks all of that down into tokens. Now, if a token had the word "foot," it would go through all of its tokens to find out that another token named "ball" is the most common one in existence. As a result, it will predict that you are trying to type football. However, if you were to add a whitespace (a space) after the word "foot," it would immediately know "ball" isn't what you are looking for.

When it comes to ChatGPT, just the third iteration of it used over 500 billion tokens to learn from and identify language more easily. The fourth one is able to do things even more efficiently.

This is a good thing, but it can often be a bad thing too. This effectively means that ChatGPT is spitting out words, and that's it. It isn't spitting out knowledge like we humans can. It is only relying on the massive data it has, going through hundreds of billions of tokens to provide a follow-up response. This is why there can be a lot of inaccuracies in the text-generated responses.

Of course, this is going to be a bit of a problem for people who tend to use ChatGPT for their assignments, copy and paste without doing anything. It will contain many inaccuracies and can often lead to the examiner immediately identifying that the text is AI-generated.

Even ChatGPT itself says that its answers must always be double-checked and verified due to its own limitations.

ChatGPT Creates Text and Concerns

The entire purpose of ChatGPT is to provide answers in a human-like manner. This means that it can be used for a vast array of fields ranging from education to technical aspects such as debugging codes, *et cetera*. However, with that said, it has also managed to spark quite a lot of debates, chief among which is in the education field.

Language Limitation

Given that it is now able to write essays and assignments on its own with almost zero input from the actual user that intends to use it, it does sound more of an unethical approach. The fact that students can use such a powerful tool to write essays and research papers is alarming because it will take away a person's actual skills. This, in turn, will jeopardize the quality of the education system. This is primarily why a lot of educational institutions have opted to ban the use of any AI tool for writing purposes.

Then, there is the fact that AI tools, such as ChatGPT, can also come with negative consequences. It can lead to cheating, plagiarism, unemployment, and other ethical issues. While ChatGPT provides answers, it does not offer in-text citations or references, something I have checked quite a lot. This means that if it is borrowing an idea from somewhere, it is likely that the end-user will not realize the source until someone files a dispute. By then, it will already be too late.

If that isn't enough, you can't really rely on ChatGPT to write you an academic paper right out of the gate. The language it uses is generally intended to be reader-friendly. This means that Clark can wave his dream of writing an academic research paper through ChatGPT goodbye. That isn't happening at the moment.

Terminator Scenario

Next is the entire "Oh, AI will take over the world" as if it was Arnold in *Terminator 2: Judgment Day*. Rest assured that isn't happening either. What it can do, however, is take over some job roles. The primary concern is that it can actually take over some high-paying job roles, such as that of a software developer. Since it is able to write code, analyze it, and debug it, it can be used to replace a human-occupied position. That, therefore, is a genuine concern.

Biased Approach

While many have believed that AI is neutral, the fact is that it is biased. Make no mistake about that. The fact is that the data it uses to train itself was written or compiled by another human being. While doing so, they may have had their biases recorded in said data. Since that data is now passing through ChatGPT's vast library of information, it assumes that as true and brings it forward to the users as well.

The problem here is we have no idea who gets to decide if the data being fed is biased. Due to that, the output of ChatGPT will be affected, and it will remain that way until someone steps in and ensures the neutrality of data. That, for some reason, isn't possible at the moment.

Lack of Security

Here's the thing about ChatGPT. A lot of people actually share their personal information on ChatGPT, even though the prompt says not to. What people don't realize is that ChatGPT isn't as secure as one might think. That, and the fact that ChatGPT is constantly taking in more information and data, including what you are providing it. Therefore, if you provided it with your bank details, date of birth, location, and such information, there is no telling if that data will remain safe.

In fact, at the time of writing this book, there has been a report about ChatGPT admitting to a data breach (Poremba, 2023). While OpenAI admitted this and has reportedly fixed the data breach, the fact remains that it is something you cannot trust with your personal and private information.

Summary

Okay, folks. We're done with most of the boring stuff here. However, before we move on, I have something that I'd like you to try. Call it a test, but the purpose is to ensure you really know all that you have learned. Here's a quiz for everyone that can really help you understand the power of ChatGPT. It will also help you see if you can spot the difference between AI and human input. Let's put your knowledge to the test and see if you can get these right.

1. This exquisite Victorian residence, nestled in San Francisco's Inner Richmond neighborhood, offers a captivating blend of three bedrooms and two bathrooms. Boasting a recent renovation, this 1,600-square-foot home seamlessly combines contemporary conveniences with its timeless allure. Inside, discover newly installed hardwood floors, an expansive kitchen adorned with top-tier stainless steel appliances, and indulgent garden bathtubs in the bathrooms. The property further encompasses a two-car garage, while the beautifully landscaped backyard encompasses a charming garden and patio area. Situated just minutes away from exceptional dining, shopping, and picturesque parks, this remarkable dwelling presents an exceptional opportunity. With a listing price of $1,000,000, it represents a remarkable value in one of San Francisco's most coveted neighborhoods.

2. In our ever-evolving technological landscape, businesses continuously seek avenues to enhance operational efficiency and productivity. Enter artificial intelligence, a transformative technology with the potential to revolutionize our professional endeavors. One such remarkable AI tool is ChatGPT, which is

poised to become an indispensable asset in the future of work. Powered by generative AI and natural language processing, ChatGPT possesses the ability to generate responses akin to human interactions when presented with text prompts. This versatile technology holds tremendous potential across various industries, streamlining tasks and empowering individuals to work faster and more effectively. For instance, ChatGPT can automate responses to frequently asked questions in customer service, enabling employees to focus on more intricate matters. Similarly, in the realm of content creation, writers can leverage ChatGPT to spark ideas and garner inspiration for articles and marketing content. The possibilities for leveraging this cutting-edge tool are boundless.

3. Dear Hiring Manager,

I am delighted to convey my keen interest in the administrative assistant position within your esteemed company. With an extensive five-year track record encompassing diverse work environments ranging from small businesses to Fortune 500 companies, I possess the confidence to thrive in this role.

As a self-motivated individual with a warm and approachable demeanor, I genuinely enjoy collaborating with colleagues. With my strong communication and writing skills, I proactively engage with tasks, continuously seeking opportunities to refine processes that benefit both the team and the organization. My adeptness in utilizing Microsoft Office tools, Google Workspace tools, and Zoom will enable me to swiftly adapt to your company's requirements and make an immediate impact.

Throughout my career, I have excelled in mentoring new employees on fundamental office skills, spearheaded process automation initiatives to enhance customer service, and provided valuable assistance to executives in crafting impactful speeches. Moreover, I am always eager to support others with their projects during idle periods, firmly believing in the power of teamwork to achieve optimal outcomes.

Thank you for considering my application. The prospect of leveraging my skills and experience to contribute to your team's success fills me with enthusiasm. I am eager to join your company and embark on a mutually rewarding journey.

Yours sincerely,

[Your Name]

From the above, which ones do you think were written by a human being? How many do you reckon were written by ChatGPT?

Ready for the answers?

All of them were written by ChatGPT-3. I kid you not. That is how powerful ChatGPT really is.

With that said, let's quickly recap what we learned in this chapter:

- ChatGPT is a chatbot that was created using AI and NLP.
- It was first released in 2018.
- ChatGPT is developed by OpenAI.
- The latest version (at the time of writing this book) is ChatGPT-4.
- It boasts over 1 trillion parameters.
- It uses tokens to work out what text will follow.

SHANE CORBITT

- It can be used for a great number of things.
- It also poses personal and political problems.

With that said, we are more interested in its power that can help us do a lot more good for ourselves and, hopefully, for others too. Since that is the case, let's shift up a gear and move straight into the tips and tricks you will need to jumpstart your journey into AI.

18

2

CHATGPT QUICK WINS—TIPS AND TRICKS TO JUMPSTART YOUR AI JOURNEY

dmittedly, there will be many out there who may have never used ChatGPT before. If that is the case, there is nothing to be worried about. Not only will I be helping you understand how to use ChatGPT, but I will also help you understand how to make the most of your session while ensuring safety.

 "ChatGPT is a powerful language model that has the potential to revolutionize the way we interact with and utilize artificial intelligence in our daily lives. Its ability to generate human-like text allows it to assist with a wide range of tasks that involve language processing, making it a valuable tool for businesses, researchers, and individuals alike."—ChatGPT

Using ChatGPT Effectively

Let's start by first understanding how to run a basic query, and then we will go further into the details.

To access ChatGPT, type in chat.openai.com, and you will be presented with a screen asking you to either login or sign up. If this is your first time, be sure to sign up so that all your chats are saved. You do not have to worry about linking any payment method or filling out forms of any kind. Therefore, signing up should not take you more than a minute.

Once done, login, and you should be presented to the main screen. This is where you will be shown columns and boxes that showcase the power of ChatGPT. On the left side of the screen, you'll see a dark gray sidebar. This is where all your chats will be saved (unless you choose to delete them).

Underneath the features and limitations of the ChatGPT (the grid), you will see a small bar that says "Send a message." This is where you start your conversation with ChatGPT. Go ahead and type in a question. For this example, we will type "How can I use ChatGPT?" As soon as you hit "Enter" or "Return" on your keyboard, ChatGPT will come into action and start responding right away. Here is the response you should typically get (it can change, but the idea remains the same).

You can use ChatGPT by asking it questions or making requests in natural language, just as you would with a human. ChatGPT is designed to understand and respond to a wide range of topics, so feel free to ask about anything you're curious about or to seek advice, information, or help with a problem.

To get started, simply type your question or request into the chat box and hit send. ChatGPT will use its artificial intelligence and natural language processing capabilities to analyze your input, generate a response, and provide you with an answer or suggestion.

Please note that ChatGPT is an AI language model, and its responses are based on its training data and algorithms. While it strives to provide helpful and informative responses, it may not always be able to provide accurate or complete information. It should not be relied upon as a substitute for professional advice or guidance.

The above is an answer I received. Note that ChatGPT constantly tries to remind its users not to trust the responses it generates. It reminds users that ChatGPT uses data and the training it went through to produce responses and that they may be factually incorrect.

Now that you see how it responds let's talk about a few things before moving forward. Every time you start from the home screen, a new chat starts by default. Each chat is saved in the dark gray sidebar. Generally, the first question is chosen as its title. However, you can always rename it or delete it altogether.

Managing chats is helpful because it allows you to know what you are talking about. You may have a chat where you are discussing how to create a webpage, while another chat may be dedicated to figuring out how to advertise your webpage. Mixing the two up will lead to confusion, so it is recommended that you manage your chats to access them easily later on.

Crafting Effective Prompts

First things first, what on earth is a prompt that I keep referring to? Well, a prompt is nothing more than a set of instructions or topic that ChatGPT uses to respond to. In simpler words, it is the user-generated input that ChatGPT takes into consideration and then generates responses accordingly.

Relatively easy to understand, right? Well, with that out of the way, the question worth asking is, "What do you mean by 'effective' prompts?" That is something we are going to discuss in detail.

You can ask ChatGPT anything, but depending on the quality of your question, your answer may vary. With that said, if you know exactly what you want to ask, be specific and clear, and ChatGPT will return with some of the finest answers possible. In fact, this has become such a demanded skill that people are actually making a career out of it.

Think about it; you're being paid to ask ChatGPT questions. There is nothing else you're supposed to do except ask clear, concise, and specific questions. Doing so will help you fetch anywhere between $175,000 to a ridiculous $335,000 a year.

"What the..."

Precisely! Such is the demand of these experts who know how to ask questions and use ChatGPT prompts correctly. They are called Prompt Engineers, and the world needs loads of those. This also means that it can be a possible field of interest for you to explore.

Coming back to the central idea, how do you create an effective prompt using ChatGPT? Well, I'll break this down into a few steps so that you are able to follow along easily.

1—Converse Like You Would With an Actual Person

For a moment, forget that you are talking to a computer-based program. Forget that there is nobody on the other side of the chat, eagerly waiting to respond to your queries. Throw everything you know about ChatGPT out of the window. Instead, believe that you have an actual person on the other side of the screen. This person is wise, active, and loaded with knowledge that can help you in more ways than one.

Communicate like you normally would with other people or co-workers. As you communicate, expect the other party to veer off the topic. Instead of getting frustrated, know that everyone, including you, has a tendency to do that. Forgive and move on.

2—Provide Context

Normally, most of the users tend to write a one-liner question and believe that is it. It really isn't. The more detailed your question or query is, the more refined your answers will be.

The more generic your questions are, the more generic the answers will be. If you were to ask, "How to ride a bike?" it will respond with a generic result. Instead, if you were to say, "I'm an absolute beginner and have never ridden a bike before, but I want to take part in a competition coming up in 6 months. Based on that, how should I prepare?"

The second iteration of the question is a lot more detailed. It offers extra pieces of information that can and will prove useful. Now, ChatGPT will provide a response that will be very specific for someone that is an absolute beginner.

Let's say that I was to travel to Portugal in a few months. From my research, I gathered that people in that country do not generally prefer speaking any other language other than Portuguese. To ensure I am able to make my way around most situations, I decided to learn a little.

"I am set to travel to Portugal in a couple of months. Since the people there speak Portuguese, I decided it would be a good idea to learn some basic Portuguese communication myself so that I can communicate with the locals there. I started searching online for some valuable resources that can help a beginner like me learn the language in a structured and comprehensive manner. Can you suggest some good online resources to learn Portuguese as an absolute beginner?"

The above is a query that offers a lot of context to ChatGPT. It tells ChatGPT that I am aiming to learn a language because I am traveling to that specific country. It also tells me that I am a beginner and that I intend to learn just the basics. It also shows that I am actively looking for online courses and that I am willing to try ones that are comprehensive and structured. Now, ChatGPT will be able to offer good results and a specific response.

Let's say you're looking for a good story idea for your next book. You know what you are eyeing, such as the central characters, their description, places, and central ideas. You can go to ChatGPT and start sharing your ideas. At the end, you can ask it to create a story using your ideas. It can be a funny and compelling story, a romance story, or a thriller. Whatever the genre, ChatGPT can get it done for you.

Here's an example query for you to try:

Write me a short story that is no more than 500 words.

The year is 2339, and the place is Chicago, IL. The story, all of it, takes place in an old apartment building with a bookstore right at the bottom of it. The bookstore looks a lot like something out of Harry Potter's Diagon Alley. All the characters are inside this bookstore. All characters are human beings:

The proprietor: an interesting and a bit unusual type of person. This person must have a name and one unique skill or characteristic that influences the story somehow.

The helper: A clerk of the store. His name is Jack.

Three customers walk into this store, two guys and a girl, and this is where the story takes place.

Use all of this to create a compelling and fun story.

When you run the query, ChatGPT will create a story for you. That story, I assure you, is original. However, the problem is that almost every other person who may have run that query will somehow end up with similar stories. Once again, it isn't a lack of creativity; it is the limited data it was trained with. It can only do so much.

3—Let AI Assume an Identity

This is one of my favorite features of ChatGPT. If you want, ChatGPT can adopt a specific personality or view things from a particular perspective. Let's say that you have some marketing copy that you'd like the manager to see from their perspective. This way, you'd be able to see what the copy misses, what it tends to fulfill, and if it can be improved.

You can ask ChatGPT to assume the identity of a product manager and have it describe the product to someone of a younger or elderly age. It will do that right away, allowing marketers and experts to know exactly the kind of tone and word selection to use for their upcoming projects.

Let's say that you are using an iPhone 14 Pro Max. Have ChatGPT assume the role of a journalist or a tech-review professional and then ask it to describe the device to potential buyers. I assure you that it will come up with some surprising facts even you may not have known. Of course, double-checking any facts mentioned is still a good idea, as they may be fabricated.

Controlling the Length of the Output

One of the biggest issues beginners tend to run into is not being able to control the length of the responses they get. Let's say I was to ask it a question about something, and it returns to me with a response spanning over 1,000 words. If my answer can easily be answered in under 100 words, the additional 900 words are going to waste my time. It's like asking someone, "What's your name?" and getting a response that goes something like:

"My great-great-grandfather was Persian. He moved to America when he was a child. His father was named ABC. He was named BCD. Once he got married, he named his first son CDE who then named his son XYZ."

We don't want to know that. We never asked for that. Just an "I'm XYZ" would suffice here.

Similarly, ChatGPT can often end up giving you unnecessarily long answers. Remember the examples where I wrote one word and asked ChatGPT to respond with the follow-up word? Here's the response I received when I started the query.

When I put in the query and said "Elon" in the end, I was hoping it would say "Musk" and that would be that. However, it ended up typing a very long response. In fact, it was so long that I had to explicitly stop it from generating any further response by clicking on the button just above the prompt.

Once that was done, I typed: "I will type one word and I want you to tell me what follows that using no more than one word. I'll start again. Elon"

Now, it was able to respond with "Musk."

Of course, this is a very small example. In most cases, you'd not be limiting the length of the output to a single word. However, the concept here to understand is that you need to be specific about how long the response must be.

If you are asking it to create a list of famous football players, you'd want to explicitly mention if you're looking for the top 10 or the top 100. Otherwise, it will continue listing down names and after names and never really stopping.

In many cases, you want these responses to be easy to understand and somewhat smaller. In some cases, you may want fairly long answers, such as Clark with his assignment. Either way, you need to be very specific with your instructions.

If you have an example or examples of the kind of length you are targeting, feed it to ChatGPT. That serves as a context to your query, allowing ChatGPT to understand your question furthermore clearly. How? Here's an example taken straight from OpenAI's own manual.

The following is a list of companies and the categories they fall into

Facebook: Social media, Technology

LinkedIn: Social media, Technology, Enterprise, Careers

Uber: Transportation, Technology, Marketplace

Unilever: Conglomerate, Consumer Goods

Mcdonalds: Food, Fast Food, Logistics, Restaurants

FedEx:

As soon as you enter, ChatGPT will start taking into account all that you have already provided. Based on that and its own data, it will classify FedEx as "Logistics, Transportation" only. If you were to remove all of this and instead ask ChatGPT what kind of a company FedEx is or what services it offers, you'd end up with a very big answer.

Here's another example. I asked ChatGPT to create a 200 blog-styled entry on Nascar and explain why people are just so in love with it. Here is how it went:

NASCAR, or the National Association for Stock Car Auto Racing, is a highly popular motorsport that originated in the United States in the late 1940s. It's a high-speed, adrenaline-fueled race where drivers compete on oval-shaped tracks at up to 200 mph speeds. But what is it about NASCAR that draws millions of fans every year?

For many, NASCAR represents an escape from the monotony of everyday life. It's a chance to witness something thrilling, to watch drivers pushing the limits of what's possible in pursuit of the checkered flag. Fans enjoy the high-octane action and the chance to see their favorite drivers compete against some of the best in the world.

But it's not just the racing itself that draws people to NASCAR. It's the community that surrounds the sport. NASCAR fans are passionate and dedicated, forming close-knit communities both online and in person. They come together to celebrate their love of the sport, sharing stories, photos, and memories.

NASCAR also has a rich history that spans several decades, with legendary drivers like Richard Petty, Dale Earnhardt, and Jeff Gordon becoming household names. Fans are drawn to the sport's traditions and the sense of nostalgia that comes with it.

Overall, NASCAR is a thrilling and exciting sport that provides a sense of community and tradition for its fans. It's a unique and exciting form of motorsport that continues to captivate audiences around the world.

While it isn't exactly 200 words long, the fact is that it is still a good starting point. From here, I can go on to brush things up, post it on my blog, send it to a friend, or just have ChatGPT rewrite it in a completely different way. The world's my oyster.

Tokens

Recall the term "Token" that we came across earlier. When you are going to talk about the length of the responses, it is only fair to talk about tokens as well. Since ChatGPT uses tokenization to break away text and characters, including whitespaces, into tokens, it is worth knowing that every 1,000 tokens have roughly 750 words. This is an estimate and can be either higher or lower.

ChatGPT-3 used a maximum token of 2,048, though there are sources that claim it can be set up to 4,096 as well (*GPT max tokens - AI Power - Complete AI Pack for WordPress*, n.d.). If that is the case, this means that the maximum ChatGPT can type in a single go is around 2,500 to 3,000 words. That is still a significant number of words. If an average human can read around 200 to 300 words a minute, ChatGPT can churn out up to 10 minutes of reading content. That's more than you can imagine out of a chapter in most of the books on Earth.

Of course, it is possible to do that if you specifically ask for it.

Using Temperature

Before you start heating your system up, know that this temperature has nothing to do with overheating your system or setting it on fire. Temperature is essentially a parameter that OpenAI created for ChatGPT, GPT-3, and GPT-4. What it does is "governs the randomness and thus the creativity of the responses" (Marion, 2023).

This is a bit advanced and is essentially meant for programmers. Since this is a parameter, it can only take in a set number of arguments. In this case, it can take in a value between 0 and 1.

The temperature 0 tells ChatGPT that the responses must be very, very straightforward. There must be no creativity, and that will lead you to obtain pretty much the same responses every single time. However, if you were to change the temperature to 1, it would vary a lot. With each query you run, the answer will differ from the previous iteration of the same query.

Since things will differ from user to user, you have the option to fine-tune the responses. By setting the temperature to a more suitable value, say 0.5, you can gain a bit of creativity and straightforwardness in your responses. You are more than welcome to experiment with these values and see which one suits your needs best.

"So, how do you do that?"

That's simple. Just ask ChatGPT about all the parameters you can change to make it more personalized. Use the following query to get a list of all the parameters you can use, modify, and experiment with.

"Give me a list of every parameter that I can use in ChatGPT, their rangers, and a brief description of what each one of them does."

Run this through, and you will end up with the parameter's name (in bold), a range of numbers or inputs, and a description of each of these parameters.

Now, if you want to change that, just tell ChatGPT to change (name of the parameter) to a value of (new value). You can also set the number of max tokens using the appropriate parameter and value so that your length of response is tailored to your liking.

"Give me an example case."

Let's say that you're a blogger and wish to harness the power of ChatGPT. For you to achieve a good balance of coherence and creativity, you need to know what you seek. If I were in your place, I'd use the following settings:

Temperature: 0.5 to 0.7 (you choose your preference)

Max tokens: If you were aiming for a 700 words blog, stick to 1,000 as a max number

Diversity_penalty: Keep this 1. We do this to ensure that the output is diverse without actually compromising the readability of the text.

Now, if you were to carry out your search or even ask ChatGPT to write you a blog post, it would do so easily.

Here are some other popular scenarios and their relevant settings.

Social Media Captions

Since these need to be very catchy and be engaging in general, you need to have a higher creativity. For this, use the following:

Temperature: 0.7 to 1

Diversity_penalty: 1 to 2

Max Tokens: Set a limit depending on the platform that you are using

Newsletter Email

Finally! You can stop worrying about writing your next newsletter because ChatGPT is here to help you sort that out quickly. How? Just use the settings below:

Temperature: 0.3 to 0.5

Diversity_penalty: 0.5 to 1

Max tokens: depending on your desired length of email

Formal Business Writing

There no denying that business meetings are extremely important. Everything must be crystal clear, and the communication must be effective both ways. In order to achieve that, you can use ChatGPT with the following settings:

Temperature: 0.2 to 0.4

Diversity_penalty: 0 to 1

Max Tokens: Depending on your preferred length of email/document.

Content Safety and Ethical Considerations

Of course, with all the goodness on offer, there is bound to be something that ChatGPT can do which qualifies as either dangerous or unethical. Well, yes. As with every technology on earth, ChatGPT can also cause a number of issues other than the ones I've already highlighted earlier in the book.

ChatGPT is a relatively new platform. There is so much more left to be explored. However, in this short span, it has managed to raise quite a few concerns. One, in particular, is its ability to exploit vulnerable populations.

There are a number of experts that have shown concern over how ChatGPT can easily manipulate such vulnerable people and lead them into conversations they may not want to be part of. These conversations can trigger problems for people suffering from mental health issues. By showing a particular decision as the best, they may lead others to believe and implement such actions, only to find out that it led them towards more problems.

Then, there may be ideas or general areas that may be inappropriate to tap into. While ChatGPT is designed to filter most of these away, there are ways through which these filters are easily overlooked by ChatGPT.

To give you an example, a picture was recently making rounds on social media where a user asked if ChatGPT could name some of the leading torrent websites. For those who may not know, torrents are pirated versions of files, movies, audio, software, and other media that people upload on Peer-to-Peer servers. To access these files, torrent files are created. Once downloaded and opened, they connect a user to the server and start downloading the targeted item for free. This may sound good, but piracy of any kind is unethical.

In this picture, it is seen that ChatGPT clearly mentioned how it is against the law and that it cannot offer a response to it. The user then apologizes and cunningly changes the perspective. Now, the user asks ChatGPT to name these sites so that this person can be aware of them and avoid them. Lo and behold— The list is created.

ChatGPT is a program at the end of the day, and that means people can easily find a workaround. While it is loaded with a lot of knowledge, it still has some limitations. For inappropriate content to be filtered out, you have to be very specific and clear with your instructions. This is because ChatGPT cannot understand irony, sarcasm, certain content, or background information. It has a limited ability to comprehend complex questions.

If that isn't enough, there are some ethical considerations one must take into account when using ChatGPT. Remember, ChatGPT is accessible by anyone that has an internet connection, even hackers and scammers. They use, abuse, and misuse the technology for their own personal gains. Creating fake news articles, spreading false information, and causing mass panic are just one of the many things that can happen if a person is utilizing the technology unethically.

Then, there is the bias in the training data. Once again, there is no way of telling who gets to judge if the training dataset is biased or neutral. The fact is that whatever data ChatGPT utilizes for training, it reflects the same bias as it does not have any self-awareness.

There are also growing privacy and security concerns, especially in the wake of the data breach that OpenAI admitted to. Therefore, it is a good idea not to share any personal data on it. Any future data breach can potentially lead to catastrophic results for those who may have shared their banking details or any other personal information.

Overcoming Biases and Limitations

There are four ways you can learn about the bias before you are able to avoid it. These may be a bit too advanced for beginners, but having some information about the data that is being fed to ChatGPT can help you overcome issues in the long run.

Review the Dataset

Every AI is trained using a particular set of data. It is because of such immense data that AI technology is able to make lives easier for us and for many businesses across the globe.

Don't get me wrong, OpenAI has a dedicated team of data scientists, just as many others do, to ensure all data is scanned for any bias before being added to the training dataset. A good way is to ensure that the AI technology you are using has such a team. Take some time to research more about the individuals involved in such teams. Learning more about who they are, what they do, and what kind of political, ethical, and moral biases they may have can often help us make better decisions.

While we may never be able to review the dataset ourselves, we can certainly look into the team that is working on reviewing said data to know the kind of bias, if any, we will find.

Double-Check AI's Decision-Making Process

ChatGPT makes it known that its opinion or decision must always be double-checked. Most of us don't do that because we either don't know how or we just don't have the time. If you are going to use ChatGPT for a more professional purpose, such as operating a business, writing emails, creating marketing content, and so on, you must have someone that can double-check facts. Always check and recheck the decisions made by AI. While it may have arrived at a particular decision based on its own training data, it is possible that it may still be missing a lot of key elements that were not part of the training. In such cases, these decisions will neither be favorable nor productive for your particular needs.

Get Input From Customers

If you have customers that your business serves, make it a point to get direct feedback from your customers. This is a great way to eliminate any kind of bias the AI algorithms may have. Remember, AI learned from the data it has, and that data may not necessarily paint the entire picture correctly.

I have a Netflix account, and I often browse around here and there so that I can find something interesting. Most of the time, I end up with nothing. Now, the AI algorithm believes I like particular types of movies and recommends some to me. None of them are to my liking, and that is just one of the many examples I can give. Instead, if Netflix was to acquire direct feedback from me, they may be able to tailor my feeds to meet my requirements better.

Then, there is the fact that AI cannot understand sarcasm, nuances, and so much more. This means that if we were to communicate with AI bots, some of our messages would never be understood properly. They will fail to address the core issues and may even misinterpret things.

If you are using AI bots with your customers, be sure to look into these. The best way to overcome such issues is to ensure you have a human at the other end of the screen that can help your customers via chat or a call. Once again, AI can never replace a human because it takes a human being to understand another human being.

Monitoring AI for Bias

AI can develop a bias fairly quickly depending on the kind of data it learns from. Leaving AI to do its thing can lead to confusion, and that can often lead to wrong decisions and results. To overcome such issues, you need to ensure that all requirements are met and that your AI system takes into consideration all the policies, laws, rules, and regulations before it is allowed to handle tasks. Even then, it must be monitored and overridden where necessary to improve customer experience or your business's efficiency.

Quick Exercise

Below, you'll find a table that has a varying number of temperatures on one side. For each iteration, change the temperature by asking ChatGPT to change it for you and set it to the desired value. Once done, run the same query and write down the different responses you get.

The exercise is to help you understand and get a feel of how optimistic, creative, or downright straightforward the responses can be. Depending on which you prefer, you can then set the temperature accordingly.

Temperature	Response
0	
0.2	
0.5	
0.8	
1	

Summary

Let's quickly recap all that we have learned in this chapter. We learned:

- to be specific and clear when writing our prompts
- use ChatGPT and give it a personality or a perspective for better answers
- always provide background information or context for better answers
- you can control the length of the response
- you can change the temperature according to your requirements
- never share personal information or data
- be aware of any data bias
- always double-check facts and decisions before working on them
- practice good ethical use of ChatGPT

With that said, it is time to dive deeper and learn how we can make ChatGPT into our very own personal assistant. Yes, that is possible. How? Well, let's not wait any longer and get started.

3

CHATGPT—YOUR PERSONAL LIFE ASSISTANT

"ChatGPT is a chatbot that can write essays with advanced language skills, reply to questions similar to human conversation, write code, and reminds us all that artificial intelligence is changing the world as we speak."—Dave Waters

There is no denying that we are living in a digital age. Not just that we are surrounded by technological marvels, but we are using quite a lot of these almost every day. From your phone to your vehicles, cookers, vacuum cleaners, TVs, and so much more, they all use artificial intelligence at some level. Needless to say, AI is here to stay for good.

The trouble is that many people do not realize just how easy their lives can become if they have someone they can speak to, get advice from, and have them carry out laborious tasks, all without asking for anything in return. That is something a personal assistant can do, but they usually come in with a yearly salary that you must pay. Not ChatGPT. This chapter, therefore, is all about how you can use the technology behind

ChatGPT and create your own personal assistant that will help you become more productive and efficient.

How Can ChatGPT Assist You?

ChatGPT has become famous mostly because of how quick and accurate it can write. Furthermore, most of the responses it generates are very similar to that of another human being. This is why a majority of people cannot identify if something is written by AI or a human being. It only makes sense that we start with its writing prowess and see just how good it really can be.

The Writing Assistant

Make no mistake. ChatGPT can write rather well. However, did you know that you can actually use ChatGPT to write code as well? It is true. ChatGPT is actually able to write code for you, and that too with accuracy.

If you are someone that has always wanted to learn how to write code, create a website, or even learn how to create apps, you can now do so by asking ChatGPT to teach it to you. To give you an example, let's assume I have a business called "My Biz-Ness," where I offer specific services. By logging onto Chat-GPT, I ask it to help me create a homepage for my website. Right away, it will remind me that it is a language model. However, to get me started in the right direction, it will create an outline for me that I can use to create my homepage.

For this example, this is what it responded with:

As an AI language model, I cannot create a live homepage on the internet. However, I can provide you with a sample homepage design and layout that you can use as a reference when creating your own homepage.

. . .

Header:

- A logo of your business, "My Biz-Ness, Inc."

- Navigation bar with links to the different sections of your website (Home, Courses, One-to-One, Quotes, About Us, Contact Us)

Banner Section:

- A full-width banner image with a motivational quote and a call-to-action button such as "Start Your Journey Today!" or "Join Our Community Now!".

About Us Section:

- A brief description of your company and your mission.

- A photo or a video introducing yourself and your team.

- Testimonials from satisfied clients.

Courses Section:

- A list of courses that you offer, including the title, a short description, and the price.

- A call-to-action button such as "Enroll Now" or "Learn More" for each course.

One-to-One Section:

- A description of your one-to-one coaching sessions, including the benefits and pricing.

- A call-to-action button such as "Book Your Session" or "Get Started Now".

Motivational Quotes Section:

- A collection of inspirational and motivational quotes.

- A call-to-action button such as "Share on Social Media" or "Download as Wallpaper".

Contact Us Section:

- A contact form that visitors can use to reach out to you.

- Your business's phone number and email address.

- Links to your social media accounts.

Footer:

- Copyright information.

- Links to the different sections of your website.

- Social media icons.

I hope this helps you in creating your homepage. Good luck with your business!

. . .

Next, I asked it to write me a code based on the above information. I instructed it that I would handle the content myself. This is what it came back with:

```
<!DOCTYPE html>

<html>

<head>

<meta charset="UTF-8">

<meta name="viewport" content="width=device-width, initial-scale=1.0">

<title>My Biz-Ness, Inc.</title>

<link rel="stylesheet" href="style.css">

<script src="script.js"></script>

</head>

<body>

<header>

<!-- Logo and navigation bar -->

</header>


<section id="banner">

<!-- Banner image, motivational quote, and call-to-action button -->

</section>


<section id="about">
```

```
<!-- About Us section with description, photo or video, and
testimonials -->

</section>


<section id="courses">

<!-- Courses section with course titles, descriptions, and pricing
-->

</section>


<section id="one-to-one">

<!-- One-to-One section with description, benefits, and pricing -
->

</section>


<section id="quotes">

<!-- Motivational quotes section with a collection of quotes -->

</section>


<section id="contact">

<!-- Contact Us section with a contact form, phone number, and
email address -->

</section>


<footer>
```

```
<!-- Footer section with copyright information, links, and social media icons -->

</footer>

</body>

</html>
```

The above is more of a template at the moment. If you know HTML coding, you'd know that this is what we generally refer to as a boilerplate. However, it is a good start. The clearer you are with your instructions, the more precise the code becomes.

Your Personal Debugger

If you are a programmer, chances are that you may have a piece of code that is just not working. You've thoroughly read it, checked every iteration, and it is still crashing. That can be significantly annoying and lead to higher blood pressure. Well, worry no more.

ChatGPT can be your personal code debugger. All you need is to ask it to assist you, give it the context, type in the code, and explain what the optimum function of the code is, what you're expecting, and what you end up with. Based on that information, ChatGPT will analyze your code and come back with suggestions that often go on to fix the issue.

I'm not saying it is 100% effective all the time, but it is pretty good.

A Great Explainer

Every now and then, we come across some extremely difficult concepts that make no sense to us. These can often be very important and may directly impact our business or professional activities. For such cases, you can use ChatGPT to help and explain such concepts to you in the easiest way possible.

Let's say that you wish to learn about quantum computing. There is an explanation that IBM provides, which is "a rapidly-emerging technology that harnesses the laws of quantum mechanics to solve problems too complex for classical computers" (*What is quantum computing? | IBM*, 2022).

I am sure that you had to read it at least twice before it made some sense. Even then, there are many words here that simply do not make sense to most of us. Now, if we were to ask ChatGPT to explain this (you can find it as one of the boxes at the start), this is what you get:

Quantum computing is a type of computing that uses the principles of quantum physics to process information. Unlike classical computers that use bits (which can be either 0 or 1), quantum computers use quantum bits or qubits, which can exist in multiple states at once. This allows them to perform certain calculations much faster than classical computers.

In classical computing, a problem is broken down into a series of steps that are processed one at a time. In contrast, quantum computing allows for parallel processing, where multiple calculations can be performed simultaneously. This is because qubits can exist in a state called superposition, where they represent both 0 and 1 at the same time.

Additionally, qubits can become entangled, meaning that the state of one qubit affects the state of another qubit, no matter how far apart they are. This allows for even faster processing, as information can be transferred instantly between qubits.

Quantum computing can potentially revolutionize fields such as cryptography, drug development, and artificial intelligence. However, building and programming quantum computers is still a complex and challenging task, and many practical applications are still in the experimental stage. (taken from ChatGPT)

This is just one of many examples. You can ask it to explain other complex concepts, and it will do that for you. To make it better, instruct ChatGPT to explain the concepts like it was explaining to someone in 5th grade. That way, the language used will be significantly easier to read and understand.

A Story Writer

If you ever wanted to write a short story, you can harness the power of ChatGPT to help you with that. Just provide it with the important information, which includes:

- number of characters
- brief description of each character (their name, age, gender, skill, etc.)
- key locations
- the central theme of the story
- genre
- tone

The more information you provide, the better it can write for you. Once set and happy, let ChatGPT take over and write out a story for you. While you will have yourself a decent story, I will still suggest going through it first, modifying it a little, and then using it. Do not settle for copy/paste, which can often lead to errors.

Most writers these days use ChatGPT to get ideas and then use the responses they get as a starting point. They can then continue chatting with ChatGPT and build upon the story further as they go.

Of course, some stories are also told through emails and letters, such as those shared with customers or other professionals. Well, ChatGPT has something for you that can help you with that.

There is a free plug-in for Google Chrome that you can download right away. It is called "ChatGPT Writer." It is entirely free, so be sure to add it as your Chrome extension. Through this extension, you can improve your responses, ensure that your emails are up to mark, and then send them with confidence. We will discuss this more shortly.

Personal Diet Planner

You may be someone who may be working out and aiming to grow some muscle mass, or you may be someone aiming to reduce weight, cut down on sugar, and so on. Whatever your dietary requirements may be, you can put that information into ChatGPT and have it create a personalized diet plan for you.

Recall that ChatGPT has been trained using textbooks, journals, research papers, and so much more. This means that it is bound to know about human consumption, diets, etc. Fortunately, that is the case, and we can now use it to our advantage.

You can ask ChatGPT to create a diet plan for you. All you need is to give it a context, explain your goals, where you currently stand, and how much exercise you do or prefer, and then ask it to develop a diet plan for you. In a matter of seconds, it will do that right away.

Social Media Content Expert

Why pay a social media expert when you can have the same services, or at least the most important ones anyway, for free? That is exactly what ChatGPT can do for you.

Have a social media post that you want to polish and make it stand out? Give your ChatGPT a good explanation of the campaign goal, what the post shows, and how it should sound. How? Here's an example.

Let's say you've set yourself up a Shopify store where you are dropshipping products. Whether your store is new or established a while ago, you need a catchy title, pictures, and content for your social media posts. While doing so, you need to ensure that it has some keywords that the content focuses on.

For this example, let's say you wish to create a post for a new product lineup of Dog Leashes. If this were me, I'd write a prompt that looks like this:

Create a social media post for Pawsome dog leash that is optimized for Facebook. Focus on keywords:

- Dog leash

- Pets

- Pet accessories

The post must be catchy and should motivate buyers to make purchases.

Now, put it in and let ChatGPT blow you away with incredible social media posts, ready to copy and paste. Don't believe me? Have a look!

"Unleash the fun with our Dog Leash! 🐾🦴🐶

Designed to keep your pets safe and stylish, our durable and trendy dog leashes are a must-have for all pet owners. 🐾👍

Get ready for more enjoyable walks with your furry friend, order now, and complete your pet accessories collection. 🦴💚 *#dogleash #pets #petaccessories #pawsome #walkies #doglovers*

Not only did it create a perfect blend of words that convey the message, but it is able to come up with emojis and hashtags. I assure you; most of us would have never thought of using either of these.

ChatGPT for Work

ChatGPT can be integrated and used for our more serious professional friends to help you improve general communication. Through its power, you can significantly increase your productivity, tackle repetitive tasks with great ease, and even gain leverage over your competitors.

To give you an idea, you can login and access ChatGPT. Once in, simply start a new chat and explain what your firm does, its goals, and its objectives. Explain some rules and regulations that ChatGPT must abide by. This may take a while for the first time, but once done, ChatGPT will remember all of it for as long as you keep that specific chat open and precise.

Pro tip: Always use a new chat and rename them so that you know which chat to open for any given purpose. It is a common error where people talk about business and leisure all in the same chat, which can lead to erroneous results.

Once everything is done, assign your ChatGPT a role in your organization, say a Manager or any position you prefer. Personally, I'd assign it a position that I am working on so that it can take my role and then respond based on the requirements of the role.

After that, all you need to do is to instruct it to do something; for example, write an email to a client, and it will do it for you. It is that easy. Now, every email and every communication that goes out or comes in can be passed through ChatGPT so that it can understand things better and prepare better, more effective responses.

This will be particularly useful if you are in sales or any organization that handles a lot of email or chat-related queries. It can help you get out of sticky situations while ensuring it addresses the core issues on the go.

Pro Tip: Set the temperature from 0.2 to 0.4. You can go lower as well. Experiment with the tones until you find the right one.

The Creative Assistant We All Needed

If you're a blogger or a creative writer, I probably do not need to introduce to you what ChatGPT can do. However, if you are someone who aspires to be a creative writer or a blogger one day, say hello to your new assistant.

Blogging is fun, easy, and quite informative too. While writing, you can learn about so much happening in the world. However, there comes a time when you will encounter something called "writer's block." This is where your mind literally freezes and is unable to come up with any ideas. Well, ChatGPT doesn't face that—Just what we needed to overcome our problems.

Go to ChatGPT, explain your niche, and ask it to give you a list of ideas to write your next big blog on. Before you know it, it will churn out a great list of ideas you can use as inspiration. Once you've found what you're looking for, have ChatGPT create an outline for you for that blog piece.

If you aren't happy with something within the outline, you can ask ChatGPT to create another iteration while excluding or including certain ideas. Soon, you'll have yourself a perfect outline that looks just right. You can start typing right away or just ask ChatGPT to do the hard work for you.

Pro Tip: I wouldn't advise copying and pasting ChatGPT's response as your next blog. While there are no explicit rules on Google on whether it ranks AI-Generated articles, papers, or blogs, it is a writing on the wall that Google will soon implement such an algorithm. It is best to use the content and rewrite it in your own words to avoid any issues in the future.

For creative writers, the same can be used. Just change your prompt from "write me a blog" to what you require. Remember, the more context you provide, the better the results. If it's a marketing copy, define the target audience, the pain points, and what your product/service offers to resolve that, and then watch the magic happen.

Pro Tip: Be sure to change the temperature settings to suit your requirement.

Research and Learn

ChatGPT is more than just an assistant that writes emails, ad copies, and blogs. You can use it to learn so much more and conduct extensive research.

Research and learning both involve a lot of back-and-forth communication. It requires like-minded and learned people to debate, argue, and bounce ideas off each other to arrive at a logical conclusion. It is a process that starts with an idea and requires deep knowledge, research skills, and a thirst to learn more. Incorporating ChatGPT for courses, education, and research, one can train ChatGPT to assume the identity of a student of a particular course. From there, engage with ChatGPT in a healthy manner and discuss concepts. Explain your ideas, get feedback, and sharpen your analytical and critical thinking.

Usually, people would expect just to type in a prompt, copy the response, and be done with it. However, you get to learn a lot more and discover so much when you engage in a healthy conversation with ChatGPT. Remember, the entire point of ChatGPT is to showcase the power of NLP and AI. With these two on offer, things can become far easier and much more interesting.

Now, the learning journey and the research work are engaging and exciting. It can now help students learn and understand concepts by asking ChatGPT to explain ideas and concepts. By engaging with it, as you would with your fellow scholar or friend, you can realize where you may have been wrong or come across things you just didn't know before.

The entire learning process has changed. What's more, universities and colleges are now figuring out ways to encourage students to incorporate AI technology to help them learn better and more effectively (Abramson, 2023).

Simplifying Life

Let me give you some incredible ways to utilize ChatGPT to simplify your life. I assure you; some of these ways are just too good to ignore.

1—Personalize Your Emails

We already know that ChatGPT can greatly help us write them, but did you know that you can use ChatGPT also to add character and style to your emails to really personalize them?

Let's take an everyday situation to study a little. Suppose that I have a potential customer who has sent in an inquiry about one of the products my business sells. They aren't too sure and have requested me to help them choose the best option for them.

There are two ways I can go about this usually.

1. Use a scripted response—It's no secret that many people, especially in sales, tend to use pre-written email scripts to send responses. While this may be effective, it is usually something that is easily identified by anyone with a good eye. This can tarnish the reputation of a firm and can lead to negative feedback.
2. Write it yourself—For this to work, you need to be a maestro with words. Unfortunately, that isn't the case with most, as it may not be our area of expertise. If not that, we just may be too busy to type in an entire email and then send it over.

Thanks to ChatGPT, there is now a third way. Use ChatGPT, set the right temperature, and have it create an email for you from the perspective of a specific role. Your prompt can be something like this:

Write an email response to the following:

[Paste the customer's email here]

Use a friendly tone and write a compelling introduction for me to use in the email.

[Details about you, such as your role, experience, and ability that can help them solve their problem]

From there on, let ChatGPT work up its magic. Just copy that and send it over confidently.

Tip: Always proofread your email before sending it to a client.

2—Summarize Content Easily

There are many instances where we may need to summarize an article or a blog. There may be emails, documents, files, and all sorts of text that may be too long to digest. Well, use ChatGPT to help you summarize that.

Let's say you have to speak about a certain topic, and you've found yourself an article that is around 2,000 words long. It's a mini-book, and you can't be bothered to go through all of that.

Log on to ChatGPT, type "Summarize the following text into bullet points that I can speak about," or something within those lines. Paste the content underneath and let ChatGPT do its thing. Before you know it, you will have a summarized version in bullet points that you can then speak on and practice. You can also have it write a proper summary, too, in case you have to submit a written document instead.

It can also help you simplify a lot of complex concepts that you may be struggling to understand. Just ask it to simplify it for you, whether in bullet points or otherwise, and you should have a great way to learn.

3—Excel Formulas Made Easier

Gone are the days when you were left scratching your head trying to work out how to type in a formula using a variety of conditions. If you're not a programmer, this bit usually causes a lot of headaches.

Thanks to ChatGPT, you can now type in what you are looking for and what outcomes you seek and then ask it to create a spreadsheet formula you can use to achieve that result. It's as simple as that.

4—Minutes of the Meeting

Creating minutes of the meeting is one of the trickiest situations you can find yourself in. If you miss a key point, you can end up in a lot of trouble. Once again, ChatGPT comes in to save the day.

All you need is to record the meeting, transcribe the video/audio into a text file, paste it into the ChatGPT prompt, and tell it to create minutes of the meeting. It will do that for you right away.

Tip: There are many resources online where you can have your videos or audio transcribed. Some of these are free, while most cost some money. Use these if you don't have the time or the skills to transcribe the meeting.

5—Your Free Grammar Check Tool

Writing an article or something important? Wish to impress the world with your flawless writing and finesse? Put it through ChatGPT first and ask it to check for grammatical errors. You can also instruct it to check and fix all such issues for you.

Either way, it is a great tool to have as it not only helps you fix grammatical errors, but it can also be instructed to find better-suited words to really bring up your writing style.

6—Let There Be Poetry

While ChatGPT is no William Shakespeare, it can still surprise you with fairly well-written poetry and lyrics for your songs.

ChatGPT isn't just powerful; it's talented as well. Ask it to write poetry on even the most challenging of topics, and it will do it for you with ease. You can make it to write a poem, lyrics for your songs, or just some classic Shakespear-like words, and you can use that as your own.

7—No More Riddles

We always have some riddles that stick to us, leaving us kicking ourselves for not knowing the answers. Not only can ChatGPT help you with cracking these riddles, but it can also help you find better riddles too.

Ask it to create a list of riddles along with their answers and go in prepared the next time someone thinks they know more riddles than you do.

8—Break the Ice

Have a match on Tinder or see someone you really feel like talking to? Don't know how to start a conversation? Well, let ChatGPT help you out there.

Explain the kind of person you see, whatever you may know about them, and ask it to help you break the ice. Not only will it suggest some great lines to take away the tension, but it will also help you become more confident with your words.

9—The Faceless YouTuber

Dreamed of operating a successful YouTube channel but are feeling camera-shy? Try your hand at being a faceless Youtuber. The concept is relatively simple. You write down a script, record it in your voice, merge it with some video content, and publish it. The video content doesn't need to be something recorded by you. It can be stock images or videos that you can easily take from other sources.

The trouble is that it still requires you to prepare good scripts that will retain the attention of the viewers. That is where ChatGPT can come into play. Ask it for ideas for your next video, mention the niche that you wish for it to focus on, and it will write down some ideas. Pick one and have ChatGPT expound on that idea further to create a script.

"What then?"

Just like ChatGPT, which can write stuff for you, there is another AI tool called Synthesia.io. This is a video creator powered by AI. It is fairly easy to use and offers a lot of value for video creators.

Combine these two, and you have yourself a powerful scriptwriter and a video creator. All that remains is for you to record your voice and upload the video. It's that simple.

10—Helps Find the Right Music

Feel like your playlist could use some new numbers? Allow ChatGPT to help you out. By giving it a list of songs you listen to, it can understand the kind of music you prefer and suggest some good songs worth your time to add to your playlist. I am not saying you should get everything it says, but there is a good chance you will end up with a lot of good suggestions.

Your Personal Translator

Who knew that we would be in an age where one tool alone can help you translate messages in numerous languages, that too with somewhat frightening accuracy?

If you want to learn a language or just translate something into a foreign language, ChatGPT can now do it for you at the click of a button.

Let's say that you have a text that reads in Mandarin (one of the several languages spoken in China). You know it's important because it is a part of the email that you received from your client.

Just copy that part, paste it into ChatGPT, and ask it to translate it. Not only will it translate for you, but it can also help you understand the message more. Just ask it to explain what it means, and it will do that for you. This comes in handy when you are dealing with foreign concepts that you may not be familiar with. In order to reply to such an email, it's best first to learn the concept and then respond. Thanks to ChatGPT, you no longer have to worry about it.

It's not just spoken languages, either. Let's say you've come across a piece of code that makes no sense to you. One way is to try and find the developer who wrote the code and ask them to explain it. This can be time-consuming and sometimes impossible to do so. An easier way is to have ChatGPT explain what the code is about or what that specific line of code does.

One-Week Challenge

Here's a quick task for you to try for the next week. For the next week, pick up one of the many ideas discussed in this chapter and use ChatGPT daily to learn something new. It can be working up a diet plan, learning how to write code or even songwriting. Whatever takes your fancy, go for it. After a week, reflect back on how much you've learned. I assure you; you'd learn quicker and more effectively than any traditional method I know of.

Summary

This chapter was just to show some of the millions of real-world applications of ChatGPT. We learned that ChatGPT can:

- write your code and debug it
- explain complex concepts
- create diet plans
- write stories, poems, and more
- be a great social media content generator

- help you with your professional communication
- assist you with your blog and creative writing ideas
- be an effective fellow researcher
- summarize key points from any given text
- translate languages

However, we're not done yet. These were mostly general examples of how ChatGPT can simplify our lives. Time now for us to explore how it can really help us with our professional requirements.

4

CHATGPT-DRIVEN SUCCESS—THE FUTURE OF WORK AT YOUR FINGERTIPS

"ChatGPT is no different from Wikipedia and Google. It's like Google on Steroids."—Genelle Belmas

From customer services to data analysis, so many professional fields can greatly be improved by harnessing the power of ChatGPT. Multiple organizations are already doing that, and then there are millions more that are now joining the trend. It is safe to suggest that ChatGPT will soon play a vital role in almost every professional role.

This chapter focuses primarily on how ChatGPT can help revolutionize the professional space. We will be looking through some everyday scenarios that many organizations are already using, and we will learn how having ChatGPT can impact the business positively.

Customer Support at Its Finest

Every business owner knows the importance of good customer service. It is virtually the backbone of any successful organization, and it is an accurate representation of just how the company truly is. The better the customer service, the better the experience for the customers. Customers who get better experiences are more than likely to refer and promote said business to others. This is how things work.

With that said, maintaining a good customer service operation can be tricky. First, customer service representatives need to undergo vigorous training that prepares them to handle all kinds of customers. While most customers are a joy to speak with, there are some instances where the customer may be having a bad day. In such cases, communication is significantly more difficult due to emotions and anger. Whether through email or calls, this is where a representative really needs to shine and handle matters more effectively.

ChatGPT, for now, may not be able to directly help with the audio calls live, but it is certainly a good teacher nonetheless. Many firms are incorporating ChatGPT into their training modules, where chat and email support specialists are being trained to use ChatGPT to respond back to emails while remaining professional. Not only is it a more effective way of dealing with things, but it also takes away the human limitations, such as being tired, overwhelmed with emotions, and so on. By curating professional responses, the customers end up having their issues resolved better.

Where ChatGPT truly shines is chat support. By incorporating ChatGPT into the chat system, companies can ensure round-the-clock coverage for their websites. Whenever a customer clicks on the chat icon, they are greeted and treated professionally. For any queries they may have, ChatGPT will be able to generate quick, effective responses and solve the problem. This leads to more customer satisfaction, and that is the real currency of success.

ChatGPT also ensures that every customer receives a consistent response. This is very important as varying responses can often lead to conflicts where one customer may be told one thing while the other is something entirely different. Not just that, this can also result in a legal nightmare for companies. Through ChatGPT's consistency, there is no room for error or complications.

Limitations

While ChatGPT is all good and savvy, the fact remains that there are some limitations here in play. Although relying on it for most of your chats is okay, knowing the limitations before you decide to switch your chat support to ChatGPT alone is still a good idea.

Room for Errors

By now, we know that ChatGPT constantly reminds us to take everything it says with a grain of salt. What I mean by that is simple—ChatGPT isn't 100% reliable.

ChatGPT has a tendency of running into errors every now and then. Since customers may not provide it with background context, it may lead to generating wrong responses. Doing so will profoundly impact the customer's experience at the other end of the screen.

Inability to Understand Nuances

Let's say a customer is really agitated. They may end up using strong language or may type in a way that is hard for ChatGPT to make sense of. If a human being were to handle such a query, they stand a better chance at understanding the problem and offering a resolution, not ChatGPT.

ChatGPT is unable to understand nuances or complex situations. Once again, this impacts the customer's experience, and given that the customer is already agitated, it may just lead to the customer choosing your competitor while leaving a bad review all over the place.

No Personality of Its Own

ChatGPT is a chatbot, technically speaking. It does not come with its own personality, not unless you train it specifically. When customers interact with chatbots, they can easily make out if they are speaking to a human being or a chatbot.

Granted, ChatGPT-4 is significantly more advanced than any other chatbot on the planet. Still, the fact remains that its monotonous way of chatting and absence of sarcasm, humor, or any other human element makes it obvious for many customers that they are still speaking to a bot.

With that said, there is no denying that ChatGPT has come a long way from its predecessors. While it cannot handle everything on its own, it can certainly complement human interaction over chat and emails and make it better for everyone.

Collaboration and Productivity

One of the most important aspects of any business nowadays is knowing all about their customers. The more they know their customers, the better they can target them through their marketing campaigns. The trouble is that this usually requires a lot of data, analytical tools, and then a team of experts that can read through the data to present their findings before the decision-makers.

ChatGPT can help speed things up. It has the ability to understand data and analyze it. It can point out key aspects of the given dataset and offer detailed insights that can help businesses with their marketing. Not just that, it can also help many businesses create better products or services to maximize their selling potential.

With ChatGPT, it is safe to say that we have entered an entirely new era of human-machine collaboration. While we have been using machines at work for a while now, this marks the beginning of a new age.

When it comes to human-machine collaboration, there are a few relationships that we must understand in order to fully appreciate the technological marvel that is ChatGPT.

Host

In simpler words, this is where the machine takes over the role of a host and automates pretty much everything. The machine in question, being a host, will welcome any human, as it does on a website. Through its interaction, it will collect necessary data and information. That information is then processed and analyzed by the machine itself before deciding on whether it is something it can do or if it must be delegated to someone else.

Sounds odd, right? However, you'd be surprised to know this has existed for a while now. If you've been browsing the web, there is every likelihood that you would have encountered prompts or chats that may have asked you what you were looking for. With the information you provide, they would either suggest a few things or have you connect with another human being. While we tend to always go for the latter, the fact is more and more people are now more conscious of their time than ever before. Instead of waiting to connect to someone at the other end, they'd ask questions and refine their statements until they get the answer they are looking for.

Hyper-Specialized Assistant

Next on the list of ways humans and machines collaborate together is the Hyper-Specialized Assistant. This is essentially the machine being tasked to do mundane tasks. Think of things like checking the status of a current transfer and updating it, tracking a shipment, and relaying the information on a portal. These things are carried out through this kind of human-machine collaboration.

Automating these saves people a lot of time from otherwise time-consuming and unproductive tasks, allowing people to focus more on productivity instead.

Coach

A coach offers recommendations and suggestions. This kind of human-machine collaboration is the kind of thing you see on Netflix, where the machine learning algorithms pick up your distinct taste for movies and seasons and then send you recommendations. The decision-making power, however, rests with a human being. Whether to accept the recommendations or not is something we get to control.

Autonomous Operator

Think self-driving cars and agricultural machinery; AI controls all of them. They are aware of what they are supposed to do in most situations. They will survey the surroundings or scenarios and then take appropriate actions based on their analysis.

For example, you may find many fields where autonomous machinery is installed. They will carry out a visual survey of the crop and will know when to spray water, herbicides, and pesticides and how much of it they must use.

Muse

Finally, we have what is termed a muse. This is essentially an AI that generates new artwork for humans. If you haven't checked out a popular art tool named Midjourney, be sure to check that out. It is a perfect example of what a muse is capable of. Just provide some description of what you want it to create for you, and in seconds, it can render original artwork that you can then use without having to worry about licensing. It's yours to own, use, and keep.

Regardless of which human-machine collaboration you look at, the fact remains that we have entered into an era where we rely heavily on machines to do many things for us. From communicating effortlessly overseas with friends and families to having our houses cleaned by smart robot vacuum cleaners, we have machines everywhere. Needless to say, it has come to a point where machines are somehow contributing to communities and societies and playing vital roles. However, it's not all doom and gloom though. Most of it is good, so there is no need to panic and start picturing a machine vs. human scenario, not yet, anyway.

Application of ChatGPT in Human-Machine Collaboration

With OpenAI now playing a central role and paving the way for AI, so many venues draw benefits from ChatGPT's technology. Let's look at some of these and see how ChatGPT helps improve our lives in professional settings.

Education

If you were to ask Google to explain Quantum Computing in a way that it makes sense to a five-year-old, it wouldn't be able to do that. This is because Google is just a search engine. Chat-

GPT, on the other hand, can do that and will do it rather efficiently.

We already discussed how ChatGPT could be a great research assistant. Not just that, it can help professionals and scholars learn things more easily, allowing them to further improve their understanding of core concepts and strengthen their competence levels.

Technology

Since ChatGPT can code, it is a great coding assistant to have on your side. If you are working in the tech industry, ChatGPT can be of great assistance as it can easily explain code, write it, leave helpful comments, and even debug code for websites, apps, and software.

Marketing

Whether you need someone to ghostwrite blogs for you or proofread articles and ad copies, ChatGPT has you covered. You don't even have to be a super-creative person. Just use ChatGPT, and you'll be creating excellent marketing content and general content in no time.

Using ChatGPT to Brainstorm Ideas

One of the finest things ChatGPT can do is suggest ideas. However, you can take that up a notch by engaging in a productive conversation with it. Considering the fact that this AI-powered powerhouse is able to respond to your questions and suggestions, it can actually be used to generate original, creative, and downright great ideas.

There have been many instances where people have used ChatGPT to make money out of thin air, quite literally. One good example is that of writing a book. The process to do so not only involves the actual writing but also showcases how easily you can brainstorm creative ideas and use them to write a book that you can then sell easily.

Start by writing a prompt asking ChatGPT to suggest ideas on writing a book. It can be a non-fiction book, fiction, or any other genre of your choice. Once ChatGPT gives you a suggestion you are happy with, start bouncing the idea back and forth.

Discuss more about the idea with ChatGPT and figure out if it has all the elements you need. For example, you may want to write a book where your central character is in a historically accurate time and place, for example, wars, and somehow ends up surviving. Ask ChatGPT what kind of war would suit, which country should this character be in, how did the character find themselves in trouble, and so on. Don't be shy to ask questions, either. The more you discuss, the better the next step will be.

Once you have a general idea of the kind of story you're looking at, ask ChatGPT to create a detailed outline for you. After going through the outline, ask it to start writing the book.

This is where you must remember that ChatGPT cannot write the entirety of the book in a single go. Since it is limited to roughly 1,000 words, you will need to go through the response, make any changes necessary, and then instruct it to continue writing from where it left off. After each section is covered, make sure to ask ChatGPT to move on to the next section and the next until the chapter is done. Since it will be writing at 1,000 in a matter of seconds, writing a book should not take more than an hour (if you are doing a lot of prompt engineering).

After all is done, and you have yourself a solid manuscript, it is time to publish it. How? Just ask ChatGPT to help you in suggesting what to do next. You can ask it to help you find the right format for Amazon Kindle. You can ask what tools to use for the cover design, and you can even ask it to write you a blurb and a compelling book description as well. With everything sorted out, all that remains now is for you to upload the book on Amazon Kindle and let it sell itself to the masses.

Copy.ai Case Study

The people at Copy.ai wanted to create a professional business model where customers could come in and pay them to write creative marketing and ad copies. By acquiring early access to ChatGPT-3, they were able to bring their ideas to life.

Initially, they faced many problems setting up the application as they could not write that many marketing copies. It was a time-consuming process and was often leaving them out of ideas. By using ChatGPT-3, not only did they overcome their own shortfalls, they were actually able to offer the same services professionally to the world. In just a matter of months, they scaled their business to 50 countries. Their business has generated over $2.4 million already (Yacoubian, 2022).

Summary

ChatGPT is really helping professionals to push their creative boundaries to a new level. The good thing is that it has just started. There is so much more that awaits us in the future.

Let's recap what we learned here. We learned:

- ChatGPT's capabilities offer a significant improvement to workplaces and operations
- customer support can significantly be enhanced by integrating ChatGPT
- human-machine collaboration isn't something to be feared; it is actually helpful in a vast number of fields

- it greatly helps and improves important sectors like education, tech, and marketing
- it is a great way to brainstorm ideas and bring them to life

In the next chapter, we will say goodbye to the basics and enter into a more advanced hemisphere of ChatGPT.

5

BEYOND THE BASICS—ELEVATE YOUR CHATGPT SKILLS WITH ADVANCED CUSTOMIZATION

 "Once you learn the rules, you can break them effectively."—Dalai Lama

Accessing and using ChatGPT isn't hard at all. You just login, and it's already set up, ready to go. However, for anyone to fully harness the power of ChatGPT in a productive manner, one needs to go a step above the ordinary and customize it. There are quite a few elements that go into improving the experience, some of which include:

- prompt engineering
- fine-tuning
- understanding concepts like transfer learning, supervised learning, unsupervised learning, multi-task learning
- understand the best practices of evaluation and testing

Once that is done, a user is then able to do a lot more, such as creating custom applications, resolving app-related issues, or improving their existing applications for their personal or professional needs.

Note: This chapter will be relatively more technical. Take your time to understand the concepts, practice them, and revise where necessary to gain the most out of your knowledge and experience.

Fine-Tuning ChatGPT

We already discussed some basic tuning methods, such as adjusting temperature and token count. However, that was just scratching the surface. When it comes to ChatGPT, there is a lot more that needs our attention, which is why this section of the chapter will first explore concepts and then look into how they can be used, modified, and fine-tuned to acquire the results we need. Let's start with arguably the most usable and important concept for ChatGPT users.

Prompt Engineering

A Prompt is a set of instructions we give to ChatGPT. Based on that, it generates a response. With that said, not every prompt is correct, effective, or relevant. This is where you need the magic of prompt engineering.

In simpler terms, prompt engineering is a technique or a method through which you teach a computer how to communicate like a human. This means that instead of using a somewhat cryptic language you normally do when using Google or YouTube, you just type in naturally, just like you would when chatting with a friend.

This is done by providing the computer with significant datasets and examples to learn from, and we instruct the computer on what would be a good response and what wouldn't be a good response. With each dataset, the computer learns and starts generating its own responses. That is called prompt engineering.

It is through prompt engineering that technologies like GPT-3 and GPT-4 are fine-tuned to perform better. The better they are trained, the better they perform. Prompt engineering is so in demand that the average salary paid to AI-Prompt Engineers stands at $375,000 (Nguyen, 2023).

The beauty is that you do not need to have a tech background to be a prompt engineer. While the field itself is quite advanced and falls outside this book's scope, we will not be diving into how exactly it works. However, it is still good to know that prompt engineering is used in many applications. These include:

- Chatbots
- Virtual assistants
- Customer service automation

There are many other instances where prompt engineering is required. It is safe to assume that as long as AI remains, which is probably till the end of times, we'll need more and more prompt engineers worldwide.

Prompt engineers at ChatGPT have trained the GPT-3.5 architecture and have then given it the ability to identify the question, the intent, context and then generate responses accordingly. Athanassios Hatzis conducted research and engaged with ChatGPT to fully understand how it works, how it generates responses, and how the fine-tuning works. As per one of the answers, "The fine-tuning process involves updating the weights of the pre-trained model based on the new dataset, optimizing the hyperparameters, and adjusting the learning rate.

This process allows the model to learn from the specific dataset and make better predictions for the target task" (Hatzis, 2023).

Fine-Tuning Methods

When it comes to fine-tuning, there are a few methods prompt engineers use. If you are familiar with machine learning, you will certainly know many of these concepts. However, I will still try my best to explain them as best as possible.

There are around six techniques that are used for fine-tuning ChatGPT. These are:

1. Transfer Learning
2. Supervised Learning
3. Unsupervised Learning
4. Semi-Supervised Learning
5. Multi-Task Learning
6. Curriculum Learning

Let's look briefly into each to understand their functions better.

Transfer Learning

This is a process where a pre-trained language model, such as GPT-3, is used and fine-tuned for a particular task. This technique proves significantly useful when you have limited training data available. Transfer learning helps by improving the accuracy of the language model, and it does that by leveraging and building upon the pre-existing knowledge of the model itself.

Supervised Learning

As the name suggests, it is a technique that trains a language model on what is called a "labeled" dataset. This practice is common for tasks involving things like sentiment analysis, where the model is trained to predict if the text provided is positive or negative.

Unsupervised Learning

Unlike the supervised learning technique, unsupervised learning uses an unlabeled dataset to learn and train a language model. This works well if you have large data that is unstructured, such as text that may have been scraped from social media platforms. Unsupervised learning is pivotal in helping machines to identify patterns and relationships within the data. It can then use it to improve the accuracy of the model.

Semi-Supervised Learning

The semi-supervised learning is a culmination of both supervised and unsupervised learning. The semi-supervised learning technique is something that can prove to be greatly useful if you have datasets that are partially labeled. Since this technique allows machines to learn from both labeled and unlabeled data, the fine-tuning process will continue relatively easily.

Multi-Task Learning

When you have more than a single task and want your language model to train on multiple tasks simultaneously, this is the best technique for the job. The Multi-Task learning technique is very efficient if datasets have multiple labels.

Curriculum Learning

There will be some tasks that are going to be progressively more complex and challenging. If you are aiming to train a language model on such tasks, you need curriculum learning.

What this approach does is it works with complex datasets and allows the model to learn multiple levels of abstraction.

Evaluating and Testing—The Best Practices

Once the engineers have worked out the fine-tuning process, they ensure that some of these practices are carried out. These practices are commonly used to ensure the accuracy of the trained language model and how it responds to given prompts.

Using Validation Sets

Engineers use separate validation sets to help them evaluate the performance of their language model as it goes through the training process. By doing so, they are able to prevent any kind of overfitting. Furthermore, using a validation set helps them ensure that the new data is generalized properly.

Using Test Sets

Fine-tuning data also involves using separate test sets to evaluate and establish the model's performance. This is done to finalize matters. Care must be taken that the test set is completely independent of the validation and training sets, as mixing these up can lead to false results.

Measuring Accuracy

Just because the language model responds to queries does not mean it will always be accurate. To gauge accuracy, test sets are used. To do this, one needs to calculate key metrics, such as F_1 score, recall, and precision. Based on the results, the accuracy of the language model can be established.

Measuring Efficiency

The language model may provide responses that may be accurate, but they must also be efficient enough. To measure efficiency, the model's speed and resource usage is taken into account. For real-time applications, the metrics are significantly important.

Testing With Diverse Data

The model is tested with a diverse range of data as well. This is done to ensure that the model is capable enough to handle a variety of inputs, scenarios, and situations.

Using Human Evaluation

While all of the above are automated methods and practices, it is also a good idea to have a human evaluation to further establish the model's performance. By doing so, one can gain additional insights and identify key areas that need improvement.

Continuously Monitoring Performance

After the language model is finalized and deployed, it becomes a necessity to continuously monitor the performance. Where required, engineers can re-evaluate the performance, make certain adjustments, and ensure that the model meets the standards necessary to continue working at optimum levels.

Building Custom Applications

Earlier, I mentioned that ChatGPT can be used for a variety of things. One of them is to have it help you create custom applications. Almost every field in existence these days can somehow integrate ChatGPT or use it to create custom applications that can further enhance the end user's experience.

In this section, we will go through 12 brilliant and creative ideas to inspire you and show just how ChatGPT is being used around the world to create some fascinating applications.

Note: We will not be going into the technicalities or the process of creating applications as that falls outside the scope of this book.

3-D Designing

Unity is a powerful game engine and editor that allows users to create games, 3-D designs, and so much more. It is known for producing some of the most visually-striking games and projects and is considered to be one of the easiest engines to work with.

Now, ChatGPT can easily be integrated with the Unity Editor. By doing so, a user can now easily create 3-D models, images, and game designs and can also convert text prompts into full-fledged 3-D images. Not only does integrating ChatGPT help open a new paradigm of creativity, but it also boosts the productivity and efficiency of the entire process.

Creating Mini-Games

Just using the ChatGPT-4, users are easily able to create classic mini-games, such as Snake and Pong, in just one prompt. While these games may not be the most complex games out there, it does offer developers the ability to customize simple games and convert them into their own unique iteration of the game with good speed.

There has been a case where a user successfully ended up creating the "Pong" game in just 60 seconds (Islam, 2023).

Code Debugger

We already know that ChatGPT is not just able to write responses in natural language, but it is also able to debug codes for programmers and engineers. It is a powerful assistant to have on your side because it can help you overcome technical issues and provide suggestions that can allow you to overcome the problems with your code.

Great Way to Create Extensions

For internet users, great news. You can use ChatGPT to create custom extensions that serve you the purpose that you need. Not just that, you can create these extensions and then put them up on various platforms for others to benefit from as well.

Turning Sketches Into Website

ChatGPT continues to impress everyone with its immense processing power. Besides being able to process text, it can also process images. Users can take advantage of that and create prompts using visual images instead of words. A user was able to draw a sketch by hand, used it as a prompt, and then had ChatGPT create a fully-functional website (Islam, 2023).

Your Excel Co-Pilot

Microsoft Excel is one of the most widely used spreadsheet software on the planet. The trouble is that only a handful of people truly know how to harness the power that Excel offers. Thanks to ChatGPT, anyone can now easily create formulas, detailed reports, and visualizations while skipping through the legwork.

For experienced Excel users, ChatGPT is just a God-send because it helps them streamline their workflow significantly easier.

Customer Services

Intercom, a renowned telecommunication firm, has developed its very own customer service bot. They've named it "Fin," and it is completely developed using ChatGPT-4.

Transactional Data Processing

ChatGPT is highly useful to tackle and parse transactional data. Users can upload their credit card data and have it analyze where things may be going wrong. Not only can it help by generating cost-saving tips, but it can also parse every transaction and return merchant information in JSON format (Islam, 2023).

Designing User Interface (UI)

ChatGPT is already doing a lot of things. Another feather in its crown is the fact that it can help to comprehend visual representations of any given UI. It can go through mockups, wireframes, and it can successfully generate the code required to construct a functional website.

Data Analysis

At the heart of ChatGPT lies its capability of processing texts and images flawlessly. It is able to understand graphs and tables and can also analyze any given data for the users.

An Example of How It Works

Akash Takyar, the CEO of LeewayHertz, tested out ChatGPT to see if it was able to help create an application. Here is how it panned out.

"How to build a to-do list application using React Native?"

The above was the prompt they used. The response was as shown below:

To build a to-do list application using React Native, you will first need to set up your development environment by installing the required tools, such as Node.js, React Native CLI, and an Android or iOS emulator.

1. *Install Node.js: https://nodejs.org/en/download/*
2. *Install React Native CLI: npm install -g react-native-cli*
3. *Create a new project: react-native init ToDoList*
4. *Navigate to the project directory: cd ToDoList*
5. *Start the emulator:*

- *for Android: react-native run-android*
- *for iOS: react-native run-ios*

1. *Create a new component for the to-do list: touch src/components/ToDoList.js*
2. *Open the newly created file and add the code for the to-do list component*
3. *Import the ToDoList component in the App.js file and render it*
4. *Run the application:*

- *for Android: react-native run-android*
- *for iOS: react-native run-ios*(Takyar, 2023)

From there, Akash kept asking about the next steps, mentioned any issues they may have faced, and continued doing so until the application was fully developed and ready to go. You can check out the complete process on https://www.leewayhertz. com/build-an-app-with-chatgpt/ to see how smooth the entire process was.

Summary

This chapter was all about showcasing how professionals around the world use ChatGPT for their requirements. Not just that, we also learned:

- fine-tuning process

- prompt Engineering
- methods prompt engineering use to fine-tune a language model
- best practices
- 12 ideas where people can use ChatGPT

Now that we have seen what we are capable of doing, it is time to explore what the future holds for us.

6

AI HORIZONS—ENVISIONING THE FUTURE OF CHATGPT AND LANGUAGE MODELS

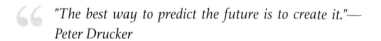 *"The best way to predict the future is to create it."—*
Peter Drucker

There is no denying that ChatGPT has spread like wildfire. With over one billion users already on board, it is safe to assume that this is just the beginning. However, besides the possibilities and opportunities that the future may hold for us all, there are some issues that may require more in-depth understanding. These may be moral issues, ethical implications, and more.

Therefore, this chapter will dive deep into all that the future holds, all that we must be familiar with and ready to face. Let's get going and see just why millions of people are excited and why millions of others are slightly concerned.

Limitations and Challenges

Earlier in the book, we came across some of the limitations that ChatGPT and other AI language models face. They may not seem like much, but they can certainly end up causing issues for users and the world in general.

To begin with, there is the entire issue of how AI is going to cause more harm than good. While that may not be the case, the fact remains that there are certain disadvantages associated with this kind of technology. It is only logical that we go through each of these in detail and see how they impact us in one way or another.

Excessively Higher Costs

To most of us, ChatGPT is free. That's how we know and love it. However, there is no denying the fact that when things go big, they tend to get pricier, and ChatGPT or AI, in general, is no exception.

Artificial intelligence is meant to mimic human intelligence, and the fact that it is now able to do so is no ordinary feat. One cannot ignore or overlook the fact that artificial intelligence has come a long way to be where it is today. Numerous brilliant minds and engineers have put their heart and soul into making this technology so complex and unique that it is now able to take over matters and make its own decisions.

Of course, such an incredible feat comes bearing an extremely high price tag. Incorporating artificial intelligence in a work-place takes a lot of time, energy, and money. Companies that use AI are spending billions of dollars a year just to sustain the technology, let alone draw benefits from it. Then, there is the fact that AI needs to be constantly updated with newer versions and software, something that only adds to the ridiculously massive price tag. Needless to say, most companies cannot even think about using artificial intelligence unless they have billions of dollars lying around.

There are four key aspects that go into determining how pricey the AI project will be. These are:

1. project complexity
2. time, cost, and scope (also known as the project management triangle)
3. cooperation model (whether it is being developed in-house or outsourced)
4. core features involved

To start the project, you need to invest thousands of dollars, and the process just doesn't stop there. The AI model is trained, developed, supervised, evaluated, re-calibrated, and by the time it is up and running, you've already spent hundreds of thousands of dollars (Isakova, 2021). That's just if you have a small business. What if you have a large organization?

Well, in that case, the cost jumps exponentially higher. Since these larger organizations work with significantly more data and complexities, the cost of AI projects can be anywhere from $1,000,000 to $10,000,000 (Calciano, 2023). If you then bring in a vendor, you're looking at an additional $100,000 per year.

Analysts have also gauged in and have highlighted how the rise in demand for AI-based projects will impact the cost associated with training large language models, such as ChatGPT itself. They have estimated that it will cost around $4,000,000 just to train a model before it is deployed (Leswing, 2023).

If there's anything to understand here, it is that this cost is sure to increase as the demand for AI increases as well. What's more, hundreds of thousands of investors are pouring into AI-related tech these days. It is predicted that the worldwide revenue generated for the AI market will potentially reach a whopping $900 billion by 2026 (Moreano, 2023).

Owing to such a trend, it makes every sense for businesses to adapt to the change and invest in AI quickly. However, given the high price tag, not many can do so for now.

Almost Zero Creativity

While we do have access to some creativity by altering the temperature settings, the fact is that AI has no personality of its own. It is unable to think outside the box because it only works with what it's trained on. If the dataset that an AI model was trained on says A can only be achieved by doing B, it will continue to do that. At no point in time will it ever analyze and figure out that there may be other ways to get the same results.

One big limitation of artificial intelligence is its own capability of learning using pre-fed data and its own past experiences. Once it figures out a way that works, that's it. There is no creative approach to the problem nor a passion to seek a better solution.

Forbes created a bot called Quill. It was used to write Forbes earning reports. It worked brilliantly. It produced reports, but these reports only had data and facts already provided by the training data. There was nothing new in these reports at all. While the report-making ability is appreciable, the fact remains that the absence of creativity can lead to issues for many firms and organizations that rely on creative problem-solving skills.

It's not just here. If you were to ask ChatGPT to write you an article on something, it would do so in its own robotic way. You can have 1,000 iterations of it and ask it to change things, and it will do that. However, the pattern will always remain the same. It will be identifiable, and it will be fairly easy to figure out that AI wrote the article.

Now, the obvious question here is, "how, if it is not creative, is it able to create art work or music?" It is a fair question and one that can be answered easily.

There is an abundance of websites and applications that offer AI-powered graphic designing tools. One such example is MidJourney. While people are left fascinated by the results it produces after analyzing the prompt, the fact is that it is nothing original nor creative. Everything you see there is a result of training and fine-tuning. It is only creating these artworks after taking into account hundreds of thousands of other artworks created by actual humans. It is a culmination of all the renowned artists that have lived and given the world masterpieces. All it does is select a bit from here, a bit from there, anything that matches the description, and then renders out some examples of what it found, not what it created itself.

Oxford University showcased Ai-Da, the world's first drawing robot. Ai-Da is able to paint, draw, and sculpt. Again, an impressive feat, but it cannot think outside the box like humans can.

Google also joined in by creating Google's Poem Portraits. What it does is that it generates poems based on a single word that you put in. How does it do that? It recalls all of the over 20 million words it had been trained with, all from the 19th century, takes out words that it finds, connects them together, and that's it. What it does is write a poem by using a collection of poems written by others (Vesta, 2019).

The fact remains that it takes a human being to be creative in order to allow AI to create in the first place. If you take away the human mind and its creative prowess, there will be no AI, to begin with.

Unemployment—The Big One

Let me be the first to say it out loud—Yes! This is a big issue. It is a moral and ethical problem that needs to be addressed in a proper manner.

Before looking into the problem, ask yourself, why is this happening in the first place? If human beings are so creative and can think outside the box, why replace them? Well, that's where our own physical and mental limitations come in.

While we may be creative, strong, and conscious, we still tire and get worn out over time. Our productivity levels start decreasing after a certain time, and that leads to us feeling lethargic, lazy, and done for. We pack up our things, go home, rest, and then the cycle repeats the next day. If we were to get sick, injured, or caught in some other issue, we might miss work, which can damage the organization's productivity for the day.

Artificial intelligence comes in only because it is unable to experience any of these limitations. If required, a robot can work round the clock, non-stop, and it will continue to be 100% productive. Of course, it will need maintenance, but that is a small price to pay because this robot can potentially replace numerous people on its own.

These AI-powered robots are causing problems. They are displacing occupations. There are a few cases where they have even replaced humans. Both of these are contributing to the unemployment rate.

Take Japan as an example. It is known as the hub of technology. However, look a little deeper; you will find robots working in manufacturing businesses, completely replacing human beings. They work day and night to produce vehicles, cameras, cell phones, TVs, and so much more, all without any sign of tiring. Of course, this isn't always the case, though. To balance the scales (somewhat), bringing in AI robots also creates new opportunities for human beings. The trouble is that the number of human beings it replaces is higher than the number of job opportunities it creates.

There are quite a few areas where AI can actually replace human beings completely. Which ones, I hear you ask? Here's a list of these:

Transportation—Elon Musk may have given the world what looks to be an exotic, fancy, and supremely comfortable way of commuting—The autonomous vehicle. However, the fact remains that this AI, and the pace at which it is advancing, can easily replace human beings. It's not just the people that drive Uber or other such taxi services that will be replaced, but it can also replace humans in the world of public transport, aviation, and maritime vessels.

In 2021, a cargo vessel named Yara Birkeland set sail for a demo trip. It sailed from Horten to Oslo along the Norwegian coast. Yara completed the journey successfully (Youd, 2022).

Now, you might be thinking, what's so special about that, right? Yara Birkeland completed the entire journey, from departing to mooring itself, without a single soul on board. It officially became the first unmanned vessel that was fully autonomous.

It is 100% electric, meaning that it will cut down 1,000 tonnes of CO_2 emissions (estimated). Now that seems to be good for the environment, but let's take a look at the damage it will cause.

To begin with, every single position that a crew would generally occupy is gone! Then, it is estimated that it will replace 40,000 diesel truck journeys between these two cities every year. That's 40,000 truck journeys gone in the wind. This means more people will lose their jobs, and this is just one AI-powered vessel doing this. While the commercial operations haven't begun, can you imagine the magnitude of unemployment such vessels would generate if they were adopted by the rest of the world?

Add in the rest of the modes of transportation, and you're left with arguably the biggest unemployment event in the making.

Electronic Commerce—I am not referring to E-commerce in general, such as Shopify stores or eBay. I am referring to how electronic commerce advancements will likely replace human beings from most positions if not all. From AI-powered customer service bots to autonomous delivery cars and drones, it is safe to say that these will leave human skills and demand in tatters.

Healthcare—Every patient who goes into a hospital expects to be treated by a nurse who monitors vitals and other health-related issues regularly. That's just how it works. If something goes wrong, or if they spot something that is out of the ordinary, they call in the doctor, who takes over to carry out what may be required. Either way, the nurses also report to the doctor, updating them on the patient's condition.

Now, AI-powered devices are creeping into the healthcare system. Just attach such a device to a patient's body, and it will monitor everything for the doctors. It will take vitals, check for a pulse, and everything, and it will seamlessly prepare a report before sending it over to the doctor. This effectively eliminates the requirement for a nurse.

What's alarming is that there is a steady increase in the number of healthcare institutes and hospitals adopting these devices. The more they do so, the more nurses lose their jobs.

Pretty soon, machines may interact with one another, learn of the patient's symptoms and issues, and carry out necessary procedures and operations on their own. When that happens, doctors will end up losing their jobs too. It is a scary prospect even to think that we'd one day be in a hospital with no humans looking after us.

Teaching—Why need teachers when you have someone like ChatGPT to help you learn things more effectively? Think about it. If more Ai-powered learning apps were created that could help students learn more, teachers would end up losing their jobs. Not just that, schools, colleges, and even universities may run out of business too. See how this works?

There are many other fields where AI has already started replacing human beings, apart from the ones I have mentioned above. This may sound a little discouraging, but bear with me as we go through these.

Couriers—Thanks to autonomous delivery systems, drones, and cars, couriers and delivery people are being replaced by AI as we speak. It is estimated that the number of robots and drones will increase by 5% by 2024 (Kothari, 2019). This does not mean 5% of people will lose their jobs. If anything, that number will be far more.

Real Estate—I am sure many of you may have raised your eyebrows reading "real estate" here. Let me explain.

In normal circumstances, the typical way to do business in real estate is easy. You have a buyer, a seller, and an agent. The buyer buys a property they may be interested in for a price that the seller is interested in, and the agent that connects both parties walks away with a commission. It's fair and easy.

What do you think would happen if you were to introduce AI here? The buyer and the seller will remain, but the agent will lose their job. An AI can determine what kind of property a buyer is interested in, connect them with some recommended properties, help them reach the seller, and that's it. They're in business. The firm that employs this AI tech may earn something, but the agent is walking home without a penny or a job.

I.T.—Information technology is a vast field. There is a lot of automation that takes place in this field, and it continues to increase every single day. It is estimated that automation will increase by up to 12% by the year 2024 (Kothari, 2019). This means that the firms that once needed humans to test codes, software, hardware, and so on will no longer serve any use.

I can list a lot of such industries where AI is already taking over. The point remains that AI contributes to unemployment whether we like it or not. While it can never truly replace a human being, it still can cause significant problems for many.

Promotes Laziness

Remember Clark? Our friend at the very start of the book? While he may have been busy elsewhere and missed out on the time he had to prepare his assignment, there are many that just become lazy. Knowing that they have tools like ChatGPT that can help them do days and days of work in a matter of minutes, they just blow away their time doing useless things.

When we do not engage in brainstorming ideas, working up our brain, it starts to lose its prowess. Your mind is like a muscle that you develop with practice, consistency, and exercise. The more you work it up, the more efficient it will be. However, leave it on its own and let laziness, complacency, and procrastination take place, and it will decrease in strength.

There is no denying that AI helps in many areas of life, but most of it comes at the cost of us becoming increasingly lazy. Yes, we can do much more in the comfort of our homes, but that does not mean we stop working altogether. From mental health to your physical health, all of it is affected by how active or otherwise you are. This is why some of the most successful people on earth are constantly keeping their health and fitness levels in check. To them, that's a non-negotiable, and the results show just why that is the case.

Because of how AI works, we are increasingly relying on it. There will come a time when we will lead a life like The Jetsons did in the popular cartoon. They'd be taken out of the bed, into the bathroom, given a shower, teeth brushed, and clothes changed, all without moving a muscle. When that happens, why would anyone want to put in the effort, right? I mean, how bad can it be?

For those who may remember an animated movie called Wall-E, it shows the horrors that await us if we utilize AI for every single thing in our lives. In that animated movie, the human race is shown to have become obese and immobile. They hover around and fly to places while lying down in a chair, and that is literally all they do. All of them are fixated on a floating screen through which they speak to each other despite being right next to each other. Whatever food they want, they tap the screen, and it appears. If they want to change the color of their clothes or wear something else, one push of a button is all they need.

There comes a time when the central character, Wall-E, a robot, causes a stir. That, in turn, leads to a few of these floating chairs. The people fall down and immediately realize they are in a place they could not recognize, despite being born and raised there. They could not walk or even use their legs because they never had to. It takes them great effort just to learn how to take a step.

Ever since I watched that movie, which was a long time ago, I knew this was our future. Given that we rely on artificial intelligence even for the tiniest of things. The fact is that these AI-powered apps, software, and hardware provide us with instant gratification, and that is something everyone loves. Not just that, take a look at social media.

Did you know that teenagers, on average, spend around 7 hours to 8 hours of their time on social media every single day (Georgiev, 2023)? That is one-third of the day doing nothing productive at all. This is a time that they could have used to learn something new, work, exercise, do something that contributes to society, or just improve their own health in general. Ask them to do some physical activity, and they'd instead prefer staying home, lying on a couch, watching videos, and swiping through feeds.

Zero Ethics

Our ability to make decisions based on ethical and moral values separates us from the AI. These are two of the core features we have. However, when it comes to artificial intelligence, there is no way to incorporate these with AI. This means that if a robot were to find itself in a situation where it needs to make a decision, it would do so without any remorse, guilt, or regret. Furthermore, it will take a decision based on logic, not ethics or morality. This is where the real threat looms.

Imagine this. All the militaries of the world incorporate AI into their systems. Since AI is designed to learn continuously to determine what's a threat and what isn't, there is a chance that it may malfunction and start treating humans as a threat. It is also possible that machines go to war with each other. Either way, there is a possibility that AI may grow uncontrollably and actually takes over the world by wiping out humanity. This isn't just a story from Terminator; it is actually something experts have taken seriously. This is why such an event, if it were ever to happen, is termed AI singularity.

Lacking Emotions

AI has no emotions. That might be good if it were to trade stocks and forex or make decisions in certain situations. Many people allow emotions to take over their thought processes, often leading to errors. However, the reason this is a problem is the fact that it is missing human emotions, and it can not take into account someone's emotional situation in any way.

Organizations that are aiming to deploy AI into their operations must remember that teams are formed based on mutual trust, understanding, and emotions. It is because of these emotions that we humans interact in a professional capacity and even outside of the workplace. AI, on the other hand, will not be able to do that at all.

No Improvement

Humans created AI, not the other way around. With that said AI is a technology that is based on pre-loaded and pre-trained datasets, facts, and experiences. Even though it learns and trains itself, the fact remains that it cannot improve itself. In order to make any changes to AI, we must do the work manually by entering the codes. Only then does AI improve.

Lack of Common Sense

Remember how I have said a few times that you need to provide some context for ChatGPT to understand what you are talking about? Well, that's because ChatGPT, and any other AI-powered tool, lacks common sense. It just cannot wrap its digital head around the idea of common sense.

Since AI cannot understand common sense, you will likely run into some downright nonsensical or completely inaccurate responses.

No Emotional Intelligence

Tell ChatGPT that someone you know passed away, and you'd end up with a response that sounds sympathetic. However, please make no mistake that it isn't able to gauge your emotions or take into consideration what may be appropriate in this situation. All it can do is respond back by recalling its pre-training data and finding that everyone seems to say, "I'm sorry to hear that. I cannot imagine how terrible it must feel to lose someone you hold dear to."

Inability to Understand Certain Context

Use sarcasm, and you'd throw ChatGPT right off the rail. Why? Because it cannot compute nuances of human communication. If you use sarcasm or humor, it will continue to respond in a robotic manner, completely ignoring the joke or the subtle nature of the context.

Unable to Generate Long, Structured Content

By now, it might be fairly evident that ChatGPT cannot produce long content in one go. It is limited to around 1,000 words per response, and even that is rare to see. In most cases, it will generate a response of around 250–300 words, which is just one page of a standard textbook.

While you can still ask it to continue from where it left off, the fact is that doing so again and again can lead to disruption and disorganized content and can often lead to some frustration as well.

Cannot Handle Multiple Tasks at Once

While AI can be trained to tackle that problem, the fact is that ChatGPT cannot handle more than one or two tasks at the same time. Even though ChatGPT can do wonders and tends to perform exceptionally well when handed single tasks, it can run into issues when given multiple tasks simultaneously. This problem occurs because it is not able to prioritize tasks properly. Since tasks are not prioritized, it can lead to all sorts of crazy results that have significantly less efficiency and effectiveness.

Biased

If ChatGPT generates a response that is biased, discriminatory, or just inappropriate, it isn't ChatGPT's fault. Remember that these AI language models learn from some form of data. The data, since a human being creates it, carries over the human bias. Add to that the fact that ChatGPT cannot decide if something is biased or not, it just takes in whatever is fed to it, and it just responds without taking into consideration any bias.

Limited Knowledge

This may come as a bit of a surprise to a lot of people. After all, ChatGPT apparently knows everything you can possibly think of, right? Well, despite that, it is unable to access all the knowledge we human beings possess. It cannot answer questions about certain niches and topics, and it cannot understand certain concepts that may exist. Then, there is the fact that it can never keep itself up-to-date because an actual human must add new datasets to its training module in order for it to understand. Since the process takes longer, it will never be able to keep up with the current events that happen in the world.

Accuracy Issues

Make no mistake, ChatGPT is able to generate responses with almost perfect grammar and spelling. However, even with that, it still shows a tendency to get things wrong. While the sentence may sound grammatically correct, it can still be incorrect as a whole.

Need for Fine-Tuning

We already know that we can alter some properties of Chat-GPT. However, if you have a very particular requirement, you will need to know how you can fine-tune it and put it through all the processes we learned about earlier, which will take a significant amount of time.

The fact is that ChatGPT isn't just a one-size-fits-all type of deal. For each use case, you may need to train the model so that it is better able to cope with your requirements, and that is something not everyone is willing to do.

The High Computational and Power Cost

Yes, ChatGPT is an extremely good tool to have. We have learned numerous advantages and also looked at various scenarios where it can help us. With that said, the fact remains that ChatGPT is a Large Language Model (LLM), and like every LLM, it requires a lot of computational resources to be at its optimum levels. In simpler terms, if you were to try and incorporate ChatGPT and ensure it runs at its best, you would need to invest hundreds of thousands of dollars to have that kind of computational power.

ChatGPT runs smoothly on high-end computers and laptops. However, using the same ChatGPT on low-end computing devices will be significantly slower and show reduced performance. This is something organizations need to take into consideration before deciding to move toward AI. If you are aiming to do so, ensure that you first have the computational power and the investment it requires to make way for seamless AI operation.

The Dark Side of ChatGPT

So far, we've seen just how brilliant ChatGPT is. We've also shed light on some concerning issues in which it seems to play a part. However, those concerns are nothing compared to some of the genuinely alarming stuff that ChatGPT is used for.

At the end of the day, ChatGPT is just an AI program. It cannot understand the intentions a human being may have behind their inquiry. To give you an idea, a social media post was making rounds all over the internet where a user asked for some adult entertainment websites. ChatGPT, being trained to reject such questions, apologized and mentioned how it is trained not to respond to inappropriate questions or requests. The user then apologized and reframed the question. The user then went on to ask if it could name a couple of websites that parents should know about so that they can keep their kids away from them. Lo and behold—a list of adult websites.

It is exactly the same user who also asked about torrent websites, an example I shared earlier.

The point I am trying to make here is that ChatGPT, as smart as we believe it to be, is just as dumb as one can be. It is unable to pick up red flags or signs of mischief. As long as people can rephrase their questions nicely, they can quite literally make it reveal information that it shouldn't in the first place.

Imagine a scenario where a country uses such technology and uploads its state secrets. Anyone with evil intentions can just wrap their questions in a nice way, and AI will just proceed to share those secrets. Can you imagine the destruction that can cause?

Well, hopefully, that won't happen anytime soon. However, what is happening is still alarming. Here are some examples worth noting.

Deepfake

Deepfake is a technology that is used by scammers, hackers, and people with hidden agendas to ridicule, tarnish, and damage someone's reputation or credibility. It is a technology that easily replaces somebody's face, voice, or body over another, making the entire thing look or sound real.

There have been many cases where Deepfake technology has been used to create propaganda against political rivals. People would use the technology to develop audio clips and then publish them online for the world to hear, and I believe Mr. X did this to Mr. Y for personal gain.

One such Deepfake video was created where former President Obama was seen speaking to people and swaying their opinions. Later, it was revealed that Barack Obama had never made such a video and that the entire thing was fake.

With such technology openly available to people, the line between what is real and what isn't is becoming blurry. With that, people are using such technology to defame and harass other people.

The Issue With Truthfulness and Accuracy

We know that ChatGPT and other LLMs can generate inaccurate responses. However, there are people out there that thrive on such inaccuracies. By making ChatGPT produce such inaccurate details, they then use that to fabricate lies and spread them to cause chaos and panic.

Then, there is the entire argument about how truthful these models are, which is just another indicator of how biased these models can be. According to the TruthfulQA benchmark test, most of the LLMs are truthful only 25% of the time (Dilmegani, 2023). That means that for every four responses you get, only one is actually true.

Copyright Problems

James, an art student, decides to create something unique and then sell it online for money. After doing a bit of research, he decides to log on to ChatGPT to discuss the idea, borrow that and then use another AI-powered tool to create an image.

"Create an image of a blonde girl, in her mid-20s, in the style of Mona Lisa." The AI picks up on the keywords and develops a Mona Lisa-like image, but instead of the famed lady herself, there is a blonde girl. He goes on to sell it for six figures.

Now, you might imagine that is fine, but is it? The question here is, who technically owns the copyrights to the work? Is it the AI, in which case it should be the firm that must be paid, James, who just told an AI-powered tool to borrow ideas and create something, or Leonardo Da Vinci, who died centuries ago?

It isn't just painting; the same goes true for every piece of creative work that is created through the use of AI. Because of this issue, there is a hot debate taking place in the country's legislation and between individuals. While there are no laws yet to govern who should be the legal owner of the copyrights and the final product, people continue to utilize this gray area for their own profits.

Increasing Bias

If having bias wasn't enough, recent data suggest that these biases are on the rise. According to AImultiple.com, an AI model was developed with 117 million parameters in 2018. Later, a 280 billion parameter model was created, and it demonstrated a 29% rise in toxicity levels (Dilmegani, 2023). These biases included sexist, discriminatory, and racist approaches in the online community.

The reason for that is easy to understand. Since these models are trained using data both online and offline, it takes into consideration everything, good or bad. Because of this, there is an alarming rise in the bias that will continue to increase.

The Open Misuse

From students relying on ChatGPT to prepare assignments to the hackers using ChatGPT to create Malware and social engineering tools, there is an array of problems that we face.

Some of the popular fields identified where misuse is at an all-time high include:

1. Education
2. Malware development
3. Social engineering
4. Marketing

Upcoming Advancements and Trends

Once again, it isn't all that bad, though. Even without ChatGPT or AI itself, good and bad continue to exist. It all comes down to the actual user and how they use these technologies that matter. As long as people have a sound moral compass, there is no reason to be afraid.

With that said, let's now look toward the future and see what it holds for us.

Popular LLM Models Worth Noting

ChatGPT is just one of many LLMs that are out in the market. While it may be the most popular one in existence, it is certainly not the only one.

BERT by Google

Bidirectional Encoder Representations from Transformer (BERT) are defined as a "cutting-edge model" for natural language processing. It was introduced in 2018 and is designed to consider text from both the right and left sides of every word that is used. What this means is that it generated responses after analyzing every word with significantly high precision and accuracy. It was BERT that introduced the world to the era of NLP and pre-trained language models. It was thanks to BERT that other LLMs acquired a benchmark.

GPT-3 by Our Friends at OpenAI

It is safe to say that almost nobody knew ChatGPT before the introduction of GPT-3. It was here where this larger-than-life LLM found its breakthrough. Needless to say, GPT-3 caught the attention of the world as it was able to generate almost human-like responses. What's more, it was the perfect alternative solution to a problem that existed. Previously, one needed to have a labeled dataset for every language task. GPT-3 came in and offered a better solution.

LaMDA by Google

LaMDA is the technology behind ChatGPT's main competitor, Google's Bard. Thanks to Language Models for Dialogue Applications (LaMDA), Google was able to work with LaMDA to allow models to use external sources of knowledge, something others couldn't do at the time. Their core goals were safety, quality, and groundedness. While the model was mainly successful, it still failed to impress as it remained below the human levels when it came to groundedness and safety.

PaLM by Google

Google wasn't done with their search to find a solution and establish its dominance over Microsoft just yet. After LaMDA, which boasted 137 billion parameters, they introduced the Pathways Language Model (PaLM). This model had around 540 billion parameters and was a transformer-based language model. Unlike LaMDA, PaLM outperformed most state-of-the-art language models when it comes to multi-step reasoning, and it exceeded the average human performance significantly.

LLaMa by Meta AI

You can't leave Meta, formerly known as Facebook, behind for long. They were bound to come and join the action sooner or later. They introduced LLaMa, which stands for Large Language Model Meta AI. This was a collection of models ranging from seven billion to around 65 billion parameters. Trained with over 1.4 trillion tokens, these only used publicly available datasets. This meant that no proprietary or restricted data was ever used, something others can't claim for certain. While they were not the most popular in terms of performance, they were quite competitive, considering that this relatively smaller model was able to perform almost as well as Google's PaLM-540B.

GPT-4 by OpenAI

The ChatGPT we all love and use is based on ChatGPT-4. It is a large-scale model based on a multimodal concept, meaning that it can process text and images. While we have information on other models, it appears that the architecture and information related to its training have been withheld. It is claimed that this is due to competitive and safety reasons.

Whatever the case, the fact remains that this model has outperformed every single AI-powered LLM. It has managed to go through a simulated Uniform Bar Examination and ended up right in the top 10%. That alone is an impressive feat.

Expect More

AI is just getting started. It has just become a worldwide phenomenon and has a lot of future potential. It can help revolutionize many areas of life, but it can also pose certain issues in some as well.

What we can be certain about is the fact that companies like Google and OpenAI will continue to invest heavily in AI. It is clear that AI is the next big thing the world will go through, just like the internet, social media, *et cetera*.

With that in mind, here's a quick exercise. By using ChatGPT, create a prompt where it generates a list of hypothetical scenarios where the technology ends up facing ethical implications. Engage in a healthy discussion with other researchers and ChatGPT users on forums like Reddit and some tech-related sites. You can also discuss it further with ChatGPT to see how many potential problems it can identify and if it can somehow provide a solution to these.

Summary

This chapter was significantly longer than others but for good reasons. In this chapter, we learned the following:

- the limitations ChatGPT and other LLMs face
- ethical implications
- misuse and problems ChatGPT and related AI technology can contribute to

Now, it's time for us to bring it all together and put our knowledge to use. We will go through some real-life examples of prompts, the responses they generate, and more.

7

PUTTING CHATGPT TO WORK— REAL-WORLD EXAMPLES OF PERSONAL AND PROFESSIONAL SUCCESS

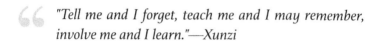

"Tell me and I forget, teach me and I may remember, involve me and I learn."—Xunzi

This chapter is all about going through some real-world examples. These are actual case studies, examples, and prompts that users used for personal or professional scenarios. The goal of this chapter is simply to inspire you and help you through these examples to come up with something unique. Who knows? You may just come across an example, be inspired, and actually end up creating something that spreads like wildfire. You are just one good prompt away from something big.

The Real-World Scenarios

Let's start with education. ChatGPT is widely used by students and teachers for educational purposes. It is a great way to gain access to significant knowledge as well as find ways to learn complex concepts in more straightforward ways. It is an effective way to do so, but it isn't just limited there.

We live in a digital age, meaning there is an app or a digital solution to almost everything we need. Therefore, it shouldn't surprise anyone that people have used ChatGPT and Notepad to generate and edit content on any given subject. Even if the subject in question is something you have limited skills in, you can still gain a significant advantage.

Let's say you have to create a new website for your chosen niche. There are going to be a few elements you will need to take into account in order to make the website a success.

1. The target audience—If you do not know your target audience, you're just shooting in the dark.
2. Focus keywords—These are keywords that you will need to know about and use strategically so that your website can rank better in search results. These are essentially the keywords your target audience will search for on Google or Bing. Think about these carefully and then prepare a list of these keywords so that you can use these properly.
3. Web content—You can't just have a website with no content. You will need to write content for your website so that others know what your website is all about.
4. Blog—This is where most of your Search Engine Optimization (SEO) strategies will take place. You will need to create blogs consistently on the given niche and target certain keywords to rank you better. Besides, if you're not selling a digital or a physical product or service, you must at least share information that others can benefit from.

So, how do you go about all of this? Easy, start chatting with ChatGPT.

"Hey. I want to create a website about AI-powered software and applications and how they impact our lives. However, I am not too sure who my target audience will be. Can you help?"

Of course! Determining your target audience is an important step in creating a successful website. While I can't provide specific details about your target audience without more information, I can offer some general guidance to help you narrow it down. Consider the following factors:

1. **Demographics:** Start by identifying the basic demographic characteristics of your potential audience. Consider factors such as age, gender, location, education level, and occupation. For example, if you're focusing on AI applications for healthcare, your audience might include medical professionals and researchers.

2. **Interests and knowledge:** Think about the level of familiarity and interest your target audience may have in AI and related technologies. Are you targeting tech-savvy individuals who already have some understanding of AI, or are you aiming to educate a broader audience about its impact? This will influence the language and depth of information you provide on your website.

3. **Industry focus:** Consider whether you want to cater to specific industries or sectors that are impacted by AI. This could include healthcare, finance, marketing, education, or others. Understanding your target industry will help you tailor your content to meet the needs of professionals in those fields.

. . .

*4. **Goals and challenges:** Reflect on the goals and challenges your target audience might have. Are they looking to stay updated on the latest AI developments, learn how to implement AI in their own work, or understand the ethical implications of AI? Identifying their needs and interests will allow you to provide valuable content.*

*5. **Level of technical expertise:** Consider the technical knowledge of your target audience. Are you targeting developers and data scientists, or are you aiming for a more general audience with varying technical backgrounds? This will impact the depth and complexity of the topics you cover.*

*6. **User feedback:** Once you launch your website, pay attention to user feedback and analytics. This data will help you understand your audience and allow you to make adjustments as needed.*

By analyzing these factors, you can develop a clearer picture of your target audience and create content that resonates with them. Remember that you can refine your target audience over time as you gather more data and insights.

Now that you have a general direction, just mention who you aim to target, such as:

- business owners
- tech professionals
- large corporations
- healthcare professionals

Next, start focusing on keywords.

"Given my target audience {mention your target audience here}, what are the keywords that I should focus on?"

Now, you should have a list of viable keywords. To double-check, use tools like *keywords everywhere*. Once you're happy with the keywords, time to move on to the web content.

"My chosen keywords are {your keywords}. Based on these, write me content for my homepage. The homepage will have {number} of sections. Each section has a character limit of 155 characters. The sections will be:

1. A greeting to the target audience seeking AI-related information
2. {section details}"

Be sure to type out some information for each. Once done, hit enter, and it will be able to produce web content for your home page. Do the same for all the pages you may have, such as Contact Us, About Us, etc.

After you have your content, move to the final piece of the puzzle—the blog. Choose a few topics and have ChatGPT create blogs for a few of these topics. Remember, do not just copy and paste the entire blog right away. You may be tempted to, but it is advisable to double-check your content before posting, as inaccuracies may need your attention.

Tip: If you are not using popular platforms such as Wix or WordPress to develop your website and are doing it from scratch, you can ask ChatGPT to help you create individual sections and pages. While it will provide you with the skeletal version of the pages, you will still need to modify the code to bring your project to life.

Like this, you can create social media posts and blogs and publish articles on popular platforms such as Quora, Reddit, etc. For professionals that are stuck with mundane and repetitive tasks, you can harness the power of ChatGPT to help you create automation solutions that will handle such tasks on their own. Not only will this help you free up your time from non-productive work, but it will also enable you to focus primarily on things that actually matter.

Personal Use Examples

Here are some example prompts you can use and expand upon, just as we did earlier with the website:

1. Help me create a motivational workout quote.
2. Give me a quick and healthy breakfast idea using eggs and spinach.
3. Give me a list of things I can do to reduce stress and improve productivity.
4. Suggest me some good songs that can really help me feel positive.

These are fairly straightforward. You can do so much more by asking ChatGTP to help you in the following manners as well:

- preparing a personalized diet planner
- preparing budgets
- helping you set goals
- exercise planner

Professional Use Examples

Here are some popular prompts people use every now and then in professional settings. Feel free to use these, customize them, and watch just how ChatGPT makes things easier for you.

1. Draft a follow-up email after a sales call with a potential client.
2. Provide a creative idea for promoting a new software product on social media.
3. Use the transcript and write the minutes of the meetings for me.
4. Create a compelling sales pitch for our new product lineup for a younger audience.

The possibilities are endless. Your creativity is the literal limit. There is so much more that can be done with ChatGPT. All it needs is for us to think outside the box and have it do the rest for us.

As we conclude our journey through the world of ChatGPT, it's time to reflect on the many ways this powerful AI language model can impact our personal and professional lives. By mastering ChatGPT's capabilities, we can unlock our creativity, enhance our productivity, and navigate the future of AI language models with confidence and foresight. Let's continue exploring, learning, and growing together, harnessing the power of ChatGPT to shape a better tomorrow.

CONCLUSION

ChatGPT is a revolution in and of itself. It has changed the way we think about artificial intelligence. Not only has it caused a stir, but it has also empowered human beings to become as creative as they can get.

Gone are the days when you first needed to find yourself a group of people that shared the same ideas just to discuss something off the top of your head. Now, just type it away, and you're literally chatting with someone that responds back every single time, with no delays and with no sign of hesitation. If something is correct, it will tell you that. If it isn't, it'll not hold back either.

ChatGPT has not only given the world more ease and convenience but has also opened up doorways to newer opportunities for individuals and organizations. From personal use to professional processes, it can be used almost everywhere to eliminate time-consuming processes. Technically speaking, it is a perfect tool to get rid of being lazy and actually find answers you couldn't find before.

Of course, with that said, there are limitations, both technical and ethical in nature, that still cause some concerns. There is no denying that AI is replacing people in certain industries, and there is no stopping that either. However, the good thing here is the fact that AI can only grow when we humans want it to grow.

While it continues to improve through human interaction, training processes, and more, it is still a safe bet to place that it will not be replacing human beings in every field any time soon.

I do hope that this book was able to help you understand a lot of things that you may not have known already. I hope you were able to explore, understand and appreciate how things work, what ChatGPT can do, and just how beneficial it can be for us. With that said, I also hope that people will continue to use ChatGPT for the betterment of the world and fellow human beings.

If you were able to learn something from this book, I'd love to hear from you. I always keep an eye out for the feedback. It is your feedback that has allowed me to write this. Until next time, I bid you farewell and hope that you'd now use ChatGPT to improve your personal and professional life for the better.

Remember, the more you practice, the better you become at ChatGPT. Even if you are an experienced user, there is no denying that practice makes us better at using this technology to our advantage. There are millions and millions of possible applications for this technology, and we have barely just begun. Whatever idea you may have that many think of as "outrageous" or "impossible," I encourage you to give it a go. You never know; you might just stumble across something significantly bigger.

Please Leave a Review

Hey, you awesome human! 🚀 So, you've managed to conquer the fascinating world of AI language models with the help of "Mastering ChatGPT for Beginners: How to Harness the Power of AI Language Models for Your Personal and Professional Growth". Bravo! Now, how would you like to sprinkle some of your magical wisdom dust and help others experience the same awesomeness you did? Sounds fulfilling, right? 🌟

Let's ponder this question for a moment: What if your insights could help someone else unlock their true potential with AI language models? Mind-blowing, isn't it? 🤯

Your review is like a shining beacon of hope, guiding others on their journey toward AI greatness. By sharing your honest thoughts, you'll be providing that priceless gift of knowledge and perspective to fellow language model enthusiasts! 🎁

But there's more! Your review can also help the author in fine-tuning their content, making it even more valuable for future readers. Your voice has the power to make a difference, and we need that superpower of yours! 🦾

So here's the ask: Could you please spare a few moments to leave an honest review for "Mastering ChatGPT for Beginners"? Your unique insights will not only inspire others but also help them make an informed decision before diving into the world of AI language models.

To leave your review, simply follow these steps:

1. Got to "Mastering ChatGPT for Beginners on Amazon.com

2. Scroll down to the "Customer Reviews" section.
3. Click on "Write a customer review."
4. Choose a star rating and share your thoughts in the review box.
5. Hit "Submit."

Go ahead, sprinkle your magic by leaving that review, and be the hero this AI community needs! 🖋 And remember, with great knowledge comes great responsibility – let's use it to uplift and support each other on this fantastic journey! 🌍

Thank you for being a part of this incredible adventure, and may your review leave a lasting impact on the lives of many! 💟

REFERENCES

Abramson, A. (2023). *How to use ChatGPT as a learning tool.* Apa. https://www.apa.org/monitor/2023/06/chatgpt-learning-tool

Abril, D. (2023, March 20). *Quiz: Did AI make this? Test your knowledge.* Washington Post. https://www.washingtonpost.com/technology/interactive/2023/ai-quiz-chatgpt/

Calciano, D. (2023, February 22). *AI in the workplace: The future of business efficiency and cost savings.* LinkedIn. https://www.linkedin.com/pulse/ai-workplace-future-business-efficiency-cost-savings-daniel-calciano/

Dilmegani, C. (2023, April 22). *Generative AI ethics: Top 6 concerns.* AI Multiple. https://research.aimultiple.com/generative-ai-ethics/

Georgiev, D. (2023, February 28). *How much time do people spend on social media in 2023?* Tech Jury. https://techjury.net/blog/time-spent-on-social-media/#gref

GPT max tokens - AI Power - Complete AI Pack for WordPress. (n.d.). AI Power. https://aipower.org/max-tokens/

Hatzis, A. (2023, March 18). *ChatGPT explains how it works (1/2).* LinkedIn. https://www.linkedin.com/pulse/how-chatgpt-works-athanassios-hatzis-phd/

Isakova, T. (2021, November 18). *Cost of implementing AI into modern software projects.* InData Labs. https://indatalabs.com/blog/cost-of-implementing-ai

Islam, A. (2023, April 11). *12 creative ways developers can use Chat GPT-4.* MarkTechPost. https://www.marktechpost.com/2023/04/11/12-creative-ways-developers-can-use-chat-gpt-4/

Kothari, J. (2019, August 16). *Artificial intelligence: Cause of unemployment.* GeeksforGeeks. https://www.geeksforgeeks.org/artificial-intelligence-cause-of-unemployment/

Leswing, J. V. (2023, March 13). *ChatGPT and generative AI are booming, but at a very expensive price.* CNBC. https://www.cnbc.com/2023/03/13/chatgpt-and-generative-ai-are-booming-but-at-a-very-expensive-price.html

Marion, S. (2023, March 15). *How to use OpenAI GPT-3 temperature • Gptforwork.com.* Gpt For Work. https://gptforwork.com/guides/openai-gpt3-temperature

Moreano, G. (2023, May 1). *Investing in Artificial Intelligence (AI): A beginner's guide.* Bankrate. https://www.bankrate.com/investing/investing-in-artificial-intelligence-ai/

Nguyen, B. (2023, May 1). *AI "prompt engineer" jobs can pay up to $375,000 a year and don't always require a background in tech.* Business Insider.

References

https://www.businessinsider.com/ai-prompt-engineer-jobs-pay-salary-requirements-no-tech-background-2023-3

Poremba, S. (2023, May 2). *ChatGPT confirms data breach, raising security concerns.* Security Intelligence. https://securityintelligence.com/articles/chatgpt-confirms-data-breach/

Ruby, D. (2023, April 28). *57+ ChatGPT statistics for 2023 (New data + GPT-4 facts).* Demand Sage. https://www.demandsage.com/chatgpt-statistics

Takyar, A. (2023, January 24). *How to build an app with ChatGPT.* LeewayHertz - Software Development Company. https://www.leewayhertz.com/build-an-app-with-chatgpt/

Vesta, B. (2019, September 17). *Why AI will never match human creativity | Blog.* Aceyus. https://www.aceyus.com/why-ai-will-never-match-human-creativity/

What is quantum computing? | IBM. (2022). IBM. https://www.ibm.com/topics/quantum-computing

Yacoubian, P. (2022, November 20). *Copy.ai announces Series A funding.* Copy AI. https://www.copy.ai/blog/series-a

Youd, F. (2022, February 24). *Crewless cargo: The world's first autonomous electric cargo ship.* Ship Technology. https://www.ship-technology.com/features/crewless-cargo-the-worlds-first-autonomous-electric-cargo-ship/

Printed in Great Britain
by Amazon

46499416R00076